Y0-CCJ-051

POLA NEGRI

THE HOLLYWOOD YEARS

TONY VILLECCO

TONY VILLECCO
TUNNEL, NEW YORK

To Barb...
Thank you for
coming to see this!.
You are
special!.
Love...
Tony Villecco
9/17/17

Copyright © 2017 by Tony Villecco

All rights reserved. No part of this publication may be reproduced, distributed, or transmitted in any form or by any means, including photocopying, recording, or other electronic or mechanical methods, without the prior written permission of the publisher, except in the case of brief quotations embodied in critical reviews and certain other noncommercial uses permitted by copyright law. For permission requests, contact the publisher at the address below.

Tony Villecco
742 Tunnel Road
Port Crane, NY 13833

Cover design and photo editing by Gene Czebiniak
Interior design by Linda Bonney Olin

Pola Negri—The Hollywood Years/Tony Villecco. —1st ed.
ISBN 1-530090016
ISBN-13 978-1-5300900-1-3

*Dedicated to Michael Heinrich, who believed in this project, perhaps even more than I did;
and to Mr. Kevin Brownlow, who inspires me with his passion
to save the glorious art of silent film from oblivion.*

1. Negri in Hollywood: The epitome of glamour.

Pola Negri brings to the screen devastating love, on the heels of which tragedy lurks.
—Picturegoer, *May 1923*

CONTENTS

PREFACE

THIS BOOK IS NOT INTENDED to be a complete historical retrospective or analysis of Pola Negri's films. Rather, it offers today's readers and film fans a fascinating glimpse into a "silent" star who lived life at full volume.

Already renowned in Europe for her talent, beauty, and passion, Negri took 1920s Hollywood by storm, making her mark in dramatic black and white, both onscreen and off. Her tempestuous love affairs with Chaplin, Valentino, and a self-styled prince—and equally rocky relationship with colleagues, critics, the press, and the fans—kept Negri in the public eye. She wouldn't have had it any other way.

Film historian Kevin Brownlow, actors who worked with Negri, and other acquaintances graciously shared their reminiscences with me. Along with news reports, other published accounts, and photographs, they shed light on Negri's unique persona and her all-too-brief career in American cinema.

I was fourteen years old when I fell in love with Pola Negri. I was staying overnight at my Aunt Marge's house and had Daniel Blum's book, *A Pictorial History of the Silent Screen*, with me. I was always borrowing movie books from our local library and had just savored my fixation with Mae West and Hedy Lamarr. But when I saw a photo of Negri, something clicked. I can't explain it—maybe it was the whole glamorous era of 1920's Hollywood and a young boy's crush—but I was hooked. She was more than beautiful, she was exotic and mysterious and something the likes of which I had never seen before.

Then I discovered her autobiography and must have read it four or five times. When I realized she was still living and residing in Texas, I spun into action to locate a mailing address. I wrote to her almost weekly, expressing my undying adolescent admiration. When a letter arrived from Texas, I was ecstatic. She, or more likely her secretary, had sent me a vintage postcard photo, not signed, but still—it was from NEGRI!

Remembering all the references to her exoticism and animal magnetism, I went to my mother's vanity, found a bottle of Tigress perfume, took one of Mom's brooches, and sent it off as a token of my love. (I don't remember if I ever told my mother or just snuck the items out of her bedroom.)

I still have the note sent to me from Negri's secretary, dated June 3, 1973:

Dear Mr. Villecco,

Miss Negri thanks you for the lovely little remembrance. She prefers not to accept gifts from fans. Of course it is impossible for her to correspond with her many fans, but she wished me to take this occasion to wish you much happiness and success in your endeavors in life.

Sincerely yours,

Myrna DeLoach, Secretary to Pola Negri

Naturally I was pleased to receive an acknowledgment, but I was also happy the gifts were not returned to me.

Thenceforth, I continued to write off and on for the next ten or so years. She sent an occasional Christmas card and once another photo. But then I got busy with other things, and Madame Negri was growing older. When she passed in 1987, a part of my childhood died with her. Movies and books and singing had all been great escapes from a sometimes tumultuous youth, and my relationship, such as it was, with Negri had been a welcome balm to a young man growing up.

For over twenty years I collected Negri memorabilia: photos, magazines, books. Twice I started to write her biography. But, as often happens in life, work and college and family matters all took away valuable time. I became overwhelmed when I would sit down to write, let alone organize, the massive collection I had assembled. Finally I abandoned the idea of doing a biography which would encompass her entire life and career abroad. Deciding to focus on only her years in America made the task much more manageable, though not without many hurdles to overcome.

About this time I had met Negri's caregiver in later years, Loretta Ellerbee. Loretta regaled me with stories and even sent me one of Negri's perfume bottles and eyeglasses as a gift; she knew how much I was enamored with her former employer.

I renewed my efforts to finalize a project which had consumed me. It was as though I *had* to finish it as some sort of exorcism, to get Pola Negri out of my system once and for all. That, of course, would never be possible. Still, I had worked too hard to not bring the book to fruition.

Negri was a larger-than-life icon, and if this book succeeds in giving readers a clearer understanding of her impact on early Hollywood and the glorious days of silent films, I will be very happy.

—Tony Villecco

Tunnel, New York

The World's Leading Moving Picture Magazine

PHOTOPLAY

February 25¢

The Greatest Issue of
Screen Magazine
ever Published

Beginning in
This Issue—
POLA NEGRI
VALENTINO'S LIFE STORY

2. Negri on the cover of *Photoplay*, February 1922.

# ONE

THE VAMP ARRIVES

If you are one of the many who delight in sugar-sweet heroines, you will not care for Pola Negri, but if you are one of the few who are fascinated by her rugged work on the screen, you will want to know more of her.

—*Photoplay*, July 1922

PROBABLY NO OTHER silent-film actress shocked yet amazed the adoring masses of the 1920s like Pola Negri. Her silent-film career in Hollywood was brief, basically 1923–1928. However, if you account for her career in Europe prior to coming to America in 1922, then she had a very substantial career, indeed.

The first foreign star to be imported by Hollywood, Negri came to America with her director, the brilliant Ernst Lubitsch. She should have had a longer career here, but there were many reasons she did not achieve the longevity other silent players were to have once "talkies" came onto the scene.

Although considered by many to be the greatest "vamp" who ever lived, Negri would balk at the characterization. What was a vamp? Is it fair to include Negri with such luminous screen vampires as Theda Bara, Valeska Suratt, Nita Naldi, Alla Nazimova, and Louise Glaum?

Film historian Ephraim Katz defines a vamp as "a seductive, often unscrupulous woman; a femme fatale." Many of Negri's screen characters were earthy and violent portrayals of women, from peasants to gypsies to chambermaids. Yet, she also portrayed queens, ladies of high society, and acclaimed historical figures. Although she always "got her man," she lost some of her exotic appeal when Paramount attempted to Americanize her, to domesticate her in roles that amused but perplexed her audiences and critics.

As early as 1921, even before she arrived in America, *Motion Picture Magazine* asked readers to select the ideal cast, which was divided into categories. The Vampire list rated Theda Bara as number one and Negri as number four, out of ten actresses.

3. The original vamp: Theda Bara, 1917.

Years later in a 1970 *New York Times* article, Negri expressed dismay at this comparison and insisted she was never a vamp. "Would you call the chambermaid I played in *Hotel Imperial* a vamp? Or the peasant in *Barbed Wire* a vamp? Definitely not. As far as I was concerned, vamps went down the drain with the market in 1929. I was the great dramatic actress."

Negri, always a study in contradiction, *did* consider herself a vamp when, in 1931, she was hoping to land the role of Mata Hari, the Dutch dancer charged with espionage and executed in France. As reported by the press, "since she won fame by playing vampire roles, she will continue in similar characters… Her first picture will be built around the life of Mata Hari." And Mata, Negri explained, "was the vamp extraordinary."

This dream was never realized. The film *Mata Hari* was later made with one of Negri's admirers, Greta Garbo, in the title role.

Negri's long-time friend and lawyer in later years, Gilbert Denman, knew her distaste for such comparisons. "All this vamp business, she didn't like it. She liked the serious role."

Perhaps screenwriter Willy Haas was relying on what he saw on the screen when he found Negri's anti-vamp protestations off the mark. "She is the vamp par excellence. If there ever was a vamp—either in Chemnitz or on the Missouri River—then she is it."

4. Pola Negri: "The vamp par excellence."

By 1922, American audiences were eager to learn more about this foreign star, who had made a huge success in Germany under director Ernst Lubitsch. Together, their films had been enormously successful, generating a buzz that could not escape American producers.

Still, with America fresh from conflict with Germany in the Great War, Negri's arrival in the United States along with Lubitsch had to be orchestrated carefully. Considering that both Negri and Lubitsch had been working for Germany's UFA Studio, Adolph Zukor, the president of Famous Players–Lasky Corporation, wished to avoid "any propagandist criticism" that might be provoked by having the two arrive together. Zukor made this clear in a telegram to Ralph Kohn, assistant secretary at Famous Players.

Negri recalled, "All that was needed was for America to show the picture and like it. The American producers wanted it, I was told, but they were not sure that their public was ready to accept a German product. Post-war Germany was not popular in the United States at the time."

That film, *Madame DuBarry*, had premiered in Germany on September 18, 1919, and immediately had been acclaimed a success. Still, it was a German film, shot at Germany's UFA Studio under Paul Davidson, head of UFA.

Writer Klaus Kreimeier stated that *Madame DuBarry* was the first postwar German film to be sold in the United States, for forty thousand dollars. It would go on to have the *New York Times* estimate its value at five hundred thousand dollars after it premiered. The huge success it was to see opened the way for other German imports. Kreimeier observed, "Thus did German film establish a beachhead in the American market."

5. Emil Jannings and Negri. *Madame DuBarry*, 1919.

Though *Madame DuBarry* was originally set for its American debut on October 4, 1920, First National sought the rights to the film, renaming it *Passion.* Because of the German connection, difficulties arose, and *the New York Times* reported that the film was "of Italian origin." This was corrected, to a point, when First National stated the film was shot in "Northern Germany with an international cast." Theaters, however, were reluctant to pick it up. Finally, the Capitol in New York agreed to premiere the film after making some fresher titles and enhancing the musical score.

So on December 20, 1920, its opening was met with raves from the *New York Times*, which called it "one of the pre-eminent motion pictures of the present cinematographic age." Samuel L. Rothafel, the director of presentations at the Capitol, saw returns of as much as $10,000 per day. The total attendance the first week was 106,000 for the 5,500-seat luxury theater.

6. Lubitsch, Negri: "I have said all there is to say about Ernie as a director. He was a genius."

It didn't take Zukor long to take action, courting Negri and Lubitsch with contracts for America. Negri was still not convinced. "I wanted to stay with UFA and continue working under that wonderful director, Lubitsch," she said. "I was satisfied with my position and making more money than I knew what to do with—about $400,000 a year. There wasn't any reason I should go to America."

And there *was* an uncertainty regarding the continued importation of German cinema. Despite Negri's acclaim abroad and the success of *DuBarry*, the October 1921 issue of *Picture Play* denounced the importance of German-made films. "Demand for German pictures, there is none. The Negri is a drawing card because she is a curiosity. She doesn't get admiring letters from girl fans, and there is little interest in her home life or her favorite flower."

This may have been the case. However, it was about to change.

The very same magazine carried an editorial by John D. Cahill extolling the virtues of Negri's performance in *Passion* and bashing the American cinema. "Call the picture propaganda—call it what you will—but you must at least admit that, in comparison with Pola Negri, our so-called screen stars appear cheap, hysterical, and amateurish."

Klaus Kreimeier placed the blame for American audiences' lack of interest in German-made films entirely on UFA: "Stars with international appeal, the kind of stars Hollywood produced, found no place in UFA's studios. In the early years, Lubitsch succeeded in promoting Pola Negri into such a figure. But then, Pola Negri was the first European actress to be offered a long-term contract in Hollywood."

So in a letter from Germany dated June 30, 1922, Ralph Kohn and Ben Blumenthal, the head of the Export-Import Film Co., Inc., raved to Zukor about the advantages of getting Negri and Lubitsch: "We know or feel that most American directors would be only too delighted to work with Negri. We are sure the stars in America would also desire to work under Lubitsch's direction and would create a sensation in America."

Kohn wrote to Zukor again on July 3, 1922, expressing his excitement regarding bringing over Negri and Lubitsch. "Lubitsch will make almost any changes we want in his contract to get to the United States to make at least one picture, and I think after he works once in our studio he will never want to come back [to Germany], nor will we want him to. He is really a great director and a real asset, particularly if he is away from the [Paul] Davidson influence. Please cable me after consulting with [Jesse] Lasky."

Fateful words! Lubitsch would stay in America and direct and produce films through 1947.

As for Jesse Lasky, vice president in charge of production for Famous Players–Lasky, he would recall the importance of both artists fondly: "Our UFA studios in Berlin were a flop financially, but out of it we salvaged Ernst Lubitsch, Pola Negri, and Emil Jannings, transplanting them to Hollywood. Not bad salvaging!"

7. A young Ernst Lubitsch.

Negri would recall in her memoirs that it was Blumenthal who first approached her and told her, "Miss Negri, you don't know it yet, but I'm going to be the one who signs you for Hollywood."

Negri immodestly claimed after the American premiere of *Passion*, "The Berlin newspapers printed dispatches saying that the Broadway audiences had gone wild over it, the first-nighters cheering and shouting their enthusiasm. Letters and cables deluged me." When she did finally sign on for America, she told a reporter she was "delighted to be back in Mr. Lubitsch's direction, since none of the pictures I have appeared in since *Passion* has been so popular as that one he directed."

Although modern Poland did not exist prior to World War I, Negri's recollections of what happened next, though impossible to validate, could have a ring of truth, despite Negri's often overdramatic and overly imaginative self. She said her allegiance to her native land, which became Poland, propelled her into departing for America. Claiming she had been vocal about defending Poland, she also wrote articles denouncing Germany's invasion during the war.

"I was suspected of not loving Germany enough in the disputes over Poles in German territory. Even the horrible word 'treason' had been whispered against me! ... Germany was in a state of extreme hysteria then, anyway, and the slightest suspicion could be blown up into enormous guilt."

Furthermore, she had been shot at and lived in constant terror. "One day I had been on a pedestal, hailed as a great artist and the savior of German films, and the next day I was cast down and trampled in the dust of rage and hate!" There does not appear to be any written documentation of Negri's frightening ordeal.

Fortunately for Negri, "America was still calling; and late in the year 1922, I set sail for the land of real freedom."

The American newspapers and magazines were working overtime in an attempt to describe this "exceptional looking woman." Her appearance was noted as "above medium height and beautifully made," with skin a "deadly sort of oyster white which somehow seems to glisten at close range." Her face was "round, rather large, though not full; there are the deep, very large, dark eyes which you notice next to the pallor of the skin; a large well-formed mouth, perfect teeth, not small; very dark hair, abundant and straight; a determined chin; an air at once executive and womanly."

Jesse Lasky told *Moving Picture World* that he planned to have Negri "make this big, special picture at our Long Island Studio." Paramount was filming in New York as well as in California. Negri did not film at the Long Island studio as reported but in Hollywood. "When American audiences see her in a powerful story, produced by a capable direc- tor,"—most likely referring to Lubitsch—"and gowned in the latest Paris creations, they will acclaim her as one of the biggest stars of the American screen."

Another vivid description, by Helen Klumph in the July 1922 *Photoplay*, made it clear that Negri was most definitely *not* like the others who had come before her. "Almost as old as the motion picture is the legend that offscreen, the vampire is a wholesome character. Perhaps that is why our homegrown vampires don't continue to thrill us. There is no make-believe about [Negri's] characterizations. There is no flinching at realism. She vibrates. She is a magnet. Crude and coarse she may be at times, but she is always convincing."

Motion Picture Classic called Negri "an intensely vivid black and white woman ... a woman immediately arresting and sure of herself ... a tropical flower cooled by the world." With such superlatives, it is surprising that Negri not only lived up to these high expectations but far exceeded them.

8. *Madame DuBarry*, 1919. Negri with Harry Liedtke as Armand.

Negri did, however, give proper credit to Max Reinhardt, from whom she received theatrical training in Warsaw. This was before the Germans ended such activity, according to Negri's interview in the September 1922 issue of *Motion Picture Magazine*. "It is from him that I learned to act, just as Ernst Lubitsch learned to act and direct under his tutelage."

Negri explained that her birth name, Apolonia Chalepez (Chalupec in later years) "seemed both too long and too difficult. So I decided to shorten Apolonia to Pola. As to the Negri part of it, the verses of [Italian poetess] Ada Negri live in my memory as one of the loveliest things in my life. I like it, and so, I hope, do my many unknown friends who know me as Pola Negri."

Negri described the death of her father in 1905 due to the "Polish Revolution against Russian rule." Later, however, her autobiography listed his death around the time she was getting to ready to film *Madame DuBarry,* which would have been 1919. She stated her mother told her of his death and that "he had the rank of Colonel in our army. He was killed in the push against the Bolsheviks. They say he was a hero."

9. Young Pola Negri.

She stated in an early pre-America interview that in 1916 she had written, directed, and starred in her first picture, which "created a small sensation in Warsaw." In actuality, she had been before the camera as early as 1914. The very early primitive film conditions in her native land, before she was approached by UFA's Paul Davidson in Berlin, propelled her interest in leaving. "I discovered that there were not in Warsaw, nor in the whole of Poland, any motion picture studios nor any facilities for taking pictures indoors with artificial lighting."

Photoplay's Maximilian Vinder wrote one of the earliest descriptions of Negri, in May 1922. He observed that Germany was bewildered as to Negri's popularity in America, but he offered his own explanation. "First of all, she was new; secondly she appeared in a 'vamp' part—a type which, having been rendered ridiculous by Theda Bara and subsequently abandoned, stood in real need of resuscitation."

Stressing Negri's unrestrained acting style, he rightfully asserted, "If she had to rave, she raved; if she had to laugh or cry, she laughed or cried. And she didn't care whether the emotion made her look ugly or pretty. She delivered the goods."

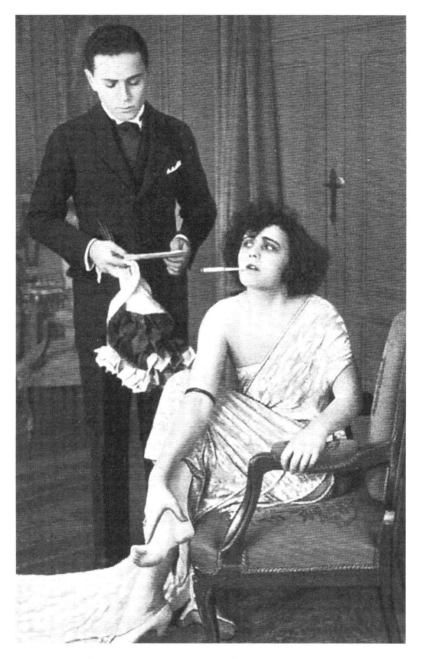

10. Before America: *Die Marchesa d'Armiani,* with Fritz Schulz.

Vinder also recognized that if Negri joined forces with Lubitsch, even more success would be achieved, as "neither is so successful individually as when working with the other." Prophetic words, as Negri's only other film with Lubitsch in America would be the successful and critically acclaimed *Forbidden Paradise*.

It is sadly correct that, while Lubitsch did go on to a much longer career in America, Negri did not. How tantalizing it is to speculate about what a film canon they could have achieved as a team in America if they had insisted on working together!

Helen Klumph's article in *Photoplay* shed more light on the mysterious Negri, with whom Americans were quickly becoming fascinated. An art student in Berlin described her as "the woman who never sleeps." Emphasizing that this was a tribute, not a reproach, he clarified, "Germans don't expect their actors to lead cloistered lives."

Indeed, the clubs and atmosphere in Berlin lent themselves to a lifestyle drenched with sexual freedom. Berlin was notorious for embracing homosexuality and bisexuality during the early twenties and before.

Louise Brooks summed up Berlin's sexual allure in her own memoirs when she described working with G. W. Pabst in the late twenties: "Sex was the business of the town. At the Eden Hotel, where I lived, the café bar was lined with the higher-priced trollops ... Racetrack touts at the Hoppegarten arranged orgies for groups of sportsmen. The nightclub Eldorado displayed an enticing line of homosexuals dressed as women. At the Maly, there was a choice of feminine or collar-and-tie lesbians. Collective lust roared unashamed at the theater."

Marlene Dietrich's daughter, Maria Riva, explained Dietrich's complex sexuality and the general atmosphere of sexual freedom in Berlin at that time, stating, "Oh yes, everyone in Berlin during that time was bisexual. Certainly Negri [was] bisexual as well." Dietrich's penchant for dressing in men's suits raised quite a few eyebrows, Riva said.

When American director and actor James Kirkwood met Negri in Berlin, he was bowled over, despite the fact he spoke no German and she no English. "Pola Negri is perhaps the most amazingly attractive woman I have ever met. She possesses more than a usual share of good looks, but this is backed up by a most powerful personality. She is vivacious, vital, gloriously alive."

Klumph concluded that Negri, "a born artist," always had to be the center of attention, a fact that would follow her to America and beyond. A star who "lives up to the traditions of artistic temperament, ... [Negri] is not modest; she is not ingratiating; she is not sweet, nor appealing. If she can't have the center of the stage at all times, she won't play ... That trait in most actors is detestable"—as Negri would later demonstrate—"in a Bernhardt, a Duse, it is part of their charm."

Actress Rubye de Remer saw Negri in Berlin and found her to be "striking."

11. Marlene Dietrich: Androgyny at its finest.

Anna Q. Nilsson, also abroad at the time, described her as "perfectly groomed," stating, "You never saw anyone look so smart … There is a flair to every movement she makes."

One of Negri's earliest admirers, Charlie Chaplin, remembered her as "the loveliest thing [he] saw in all Europe." He stated she was "really beautiful, in a typical Polish way, with jet-black hair, very small white teeth, and warm coloring."

Is it any wonder that American moviegoers were fascinated by learning more about this "tropical flower"?

So on September 6, 1922, Negri boarded the *Majestic*, heading for a new world. As she still spoke no English, what lay ahead would prove interesting, indeed.

"I climbed aboard with my twenty-seven trunks and my French maid. Hundreds of fans waved as I sailed toward New York," she later recalled. "I was newly bewildered to realize my French maid could not speak English and the Scotchman who had tutored me in English had inadvertently taught me his thick burr."

The ship's manifest for "alien passengers" sailing on September 6, 1922, recorded that an Apollonia [Countess] Domska was aboard and that she was able to speak English, French, German, Russian, and Polish. Negri, who had married so-called Count Eugene Domski while in Warsaw, stated before her arrival in America that the marriage had proved "unhappy," and after having lived with him a year she had "decided to secure a divorce." Why she entered the United States as Countess Domska remains an enigma.

Celebrities often like to deduct several years from their true age; so did Negri. Much later, when her career was over, she told the *American Weekly*, "I came to Hollywood at seventeen as a screen star." According to her actual birth record, as well as the *Majestic*'s manifest, she would have been twenty-five.

To further illustrate Negri's inconsistencies in her own stories, she expressed excitement, and yet disappointment in a separate interview, when learning aboard ship that her first American film would be *Bella Donna*, based on the Robert Hichens novel.

"The Paramount Company had great plans for this picture. I was given to understand, and it was expected, that I would be a 'knockout' in it and 'clean up,' two terms that I didn't understand, but I knew they must mean a sweeping success."

And yet, *Motion Picture Magazine* quoted Negri in December of 1922 as being less than excited. "When zey meet me at ze steamer and say you are to do *Bella Donna*, I felt like cry … I don' like to play bad women all ze time." Years later, in her autobiography, she recalled, "I did not feel that my first role in this country should be of another woman devoid of morals … It would be terrible if Hollywood thought of me in only terms of playing vamps."

Ben Blumenthal accompanied Negri on board the *Majestic* and encouraged her to mingle on the ship to hype up publicity. Hesitant to do so, she decided to stay in her cabin because, according to her, "the fewer appearances you make, the more they talk about you."

Another inconsistency in Negri's memoirs was her statement that she did not meet actress Mabel Normand, who also was a passenger, on board the ship. Negri said she later regretted not having had that opportunity, as she admired "the talents of this brilliant comedienne."

Hedda Hopper recounted Normand's version of the ship's crossing. In this history,

Normand did meet Negri and told her how to behave once she arrived in Hollywood: If the studio were to offer Negri anything but the best, she must say no. Actually, her advice was to say no to almost any and everything, as "that's the way a great star acts." If Negri would comply with these instructions, Normand told her bluntly, she would "be greater than Gloria Swanson."

Ironically, Negri and Swanson would soon appear to engage in a feud—two great stars at the same studio.

As soon as the ship stopped at Ellis Island on September 12, 1922, Negri was greeted by native Polish Americans singing and waving banners. "I was the first motion picture star imported to America, and it seemed that all New York turned out to welcome me," she recalled.

Pola Negri

12. Negri. Acclaimed in Germany, wooed by America.

Reporters swarmed the ship. Negri still spoke very little English, but she remembered that it made no difference, because "they had not only come prepared with questions but with my answers too."

After a whirlwind tour of New York, she was driven to the Hotel St. Regis, where she would stay until her departure for California.

The following day Negri was fêted at a fashionable restaurant, Louis Sherry's, where she met nearly one hundred representatives of New York newspapers and national publications. She was introduced by Adolph Zukor, with Ben Blumenthal trying to serve as translator. Negri was appreciative of the warm reception but regretted that "she could not express herself well in English."

Moving Picture World described her as "a feminine D'Artagnan. She is quiet, even serious, until she speaks. Then her freshness and enthusiasm come to the surface, and she is modestly animated."

Once she was settled in her hotel, interviews were scheduled with various film magazines. One in particular is worth repeating, as it gives an indication of the persona Negri was developing. Furthermore, it shows some of the exotic traits that would enthrall the press until she lost favor with the moviegoing public.

Gladys Hall and Adele Fletcher wrote in *Motion Picture Magazine*, "You have always wanted to see temperament in action… I do not doubt the great Continental star will manifest it. Her press department has assured me of that. She has already refused to grant more interviews than she has given. She has broken scores of appointments with photographers."

After a back-and-forth between the two women reporters and Negri's entourage, she agreed to grant them an audience, but not until she'd made them wait a considerable time in her suite. The moment of her arrival, however, was worth the anticipation.

"There stands The Negri… something of a vision; her blue-black hair is brushed severely back from her white, white face and bound about with a vivid jade green ribbon. Her lips are a vivid vermilion… She is a composite of all the great sirens of history and legend."

"Ver' nice of you to come. I have been so seeck," said Negri. "All day I see nobody. Ze offices—zey make arrangement for me to be what you call photographed—and I do not go. Go, go, go, always in America you go. Ver' nice, but ver', ver' tiresome."

The two reporters pressed on with questions. How does Negri like America? American men? Charlie Chaplin?

Negri replied:

Amerika men! Ver' much. Zey are what you say—healthy animals. And zey are what you call sportsmanlike. Zey are wirile.

Ah, Charlie Chaplin. He is ze great artist. And as just ze man—he is great, too. When I get to California I see him again.

In California I shall have a leetle house wiz a beeg garden. An' I shall have a ver', ver' good cook. Food, I like ver' much. 'Specially Polish cooking … I like to eat.

You laugh at my Eenglish? What I say wrong? When I come back from California you will be surprised at Pola Negri. She will speak to you like an Amerika.

Negri left more than just an impression on her audience. They thought her not only beautiful but "fascinating … dangerous … very dangerous. I wouldn't like to have her for an enemy," said Hall.

"Alas for Hollywood! Alas for the Amerika men!" said Fletcher.

"Alas for the Amerika women," added Hall. "They may as well go into permanent retreat."

The vamp had arrived.

AUGUST 25¢

Classic

A BREWSTER PUBLICATION

13. Negri on the cover of *Motion Picture Classic*, August 1923.

# TWO

PERILS WITH POLA

Fits of hysteria weren't encouraged by the studio, but were certainly tolerated. Pola, at the drop of a false eyelash, would sail majestically off a set …

One day with six thousand extras waiting on a location set, Miss Negri decided that she could not possibly appear.

—Howard Greer, *Town and Country*, November 1950

FILM HISTORIAN AND WRITER William K. Everson best described Pola Negri's appeal and the reason why her entry into American cinema was so dramatic. He saluted Negri's earthy passion and vitality. "In an age of Pickfords and Gishes, [Negri] brought a much-needed note of honesty and reality into the star system."

To better understand the temperament of the 1920s silent-film stars, particularly one as explosive as Pola Negri, one has to look at that era as a whole. In an age of F. Scott Fitzgerald, whose writings captured 1920s America, the new and growing art of silent film would shape a nation. This decade was a time of divine madness, guilt-free excess, and a driving energy no other era had equaled.

The tumultuous time of Prohibition, bootleg booze, a freer attitude toward love and sex, and the new music—jazz—propelled Americans (at least those who were willing) into one decade-long fantastic and frenzied dance party. Criminals were somewhat idolized. Lindbergh's transatlantic crossing to Paris mesmerized a nation. Baseball's Babe Ruth became a household name. These were a few jewels in the crown of an age filled with decadence, drugs (opium dens were plentiful), and flat-chested women dancing the Charleston.

Raccoon coats, Rudy Vallée, and collegiate sports heroes commanded attention. Women wore shorter skirts, bobbed their hair, and flaunted cigarettes, showing an almost defiant attitude.

Archivist and historian James Card summed up the period. "In the mid-1920s they ran up the banner of a new slogan: Eat, drink, and be nasty."

14. Negri meets Babe Ruth. April 1925.

Now add a new Hollywood with its beautiful people, daring people, emulated people, and morally corrupt people, and one gets a clearer sense of why Pola Negri represented a tantalizing yet unapproachable pinnacle to her adoring early fans and, yes, her rivals.

Fresh from World War I, adoring fans idolized and emulated the burgeoning stars of silent film. Hollywood in the '20s was a place of glamorous excess. The public demanded it, and the stars seldom let them down, especially Negri. Columns were written about the thick white cream delivered to her house for her daily bath—five gallons every morning!

Negri recalled, "Everyone in Europe regarded Hollywood in terms of wild parties and fantastic orgies, where money was just thrown about." She remembered the automobiles that stars had specially designed for themselves. "Fatty Arbuckle's cost $25,000"—a fortune during the '20s. "Tom Mix had a white car with steer horns on the radiator and his name in big letters on each door." As for Negri, the studio insisted her car must have "ermine fittings and a large ermine lap robe."

Adolphe Menjou recalled that Rudolph Valentino initially bought a secondhand Fiat "as ornate as a gondola," but when Valentino became a hit he purchased an $18,000 Isotta Franchini. Chaplin bought a Locomobile that could seat twelve. When he sat alone in the back seat, he resembled, according to Menjou, "Tom Thumb in an oversize bathtub."

15. Adolphe Menjou: Negri's co-star in several films.

Even the young collegiate actor David Rollins sported a little roadster that he named CLARA BOW after his favorite star, because "it had wheels the same color of her hair."

Such were the many extravagances of early Hollywood. "I thought that unless I had a car half a block long, I would be considered a vagrant," Menjou remembered.

Negri stood apart from the other stars because she was European and much more of a novelty than homegrown American women were. As she was the first European actress to be invited to America, people were naturally curious about her appeal, just as they would later become enamored with Greta Garbo and Marlene Dietrich, two other European imports. Although other foreign actors and actresses eventually arrived in America by the hundreds in the 1920s, Negri was the first whose exotic persona added to that mysterious and forever-glamorous time.

Early Hollywood scenarist Frances Marion recalled in her own memoirs the potent effect Negri had on her male followers. "Young men talked about her like amateur poets, while elderly gents hied themselves to Max Factor's and were fitted with toupees. Such was the devastating effect on our males when 'La Negri' descended upon Hollywood."

Even Greta Garbo was reportedly a fan of Negri. Grey Horan, great-niece to Garbo, though not at liberty to quote directly from Garbo's correspondences, recalled that Garbo had mentioned "Mauritz Stiller was with Lasky and handling Pola Negri, who was supposed to be very stylish."

16. *Hotel Imperial* set, 1927. Negri, producer Erich Pommer, director Mauritz Stiller.

Negri was, if not the most, certainly one of the most beautiful and talked-about women in America, thanks to an ever-present flair for the press. The time was one she would later recall as "youth and exhilaration."

Negri was not the only star to recognize that she had achieved such prominence partly *because* of the time in which she had arrived. Actress Madge Bellamy, a Negri admirer, was voted eleventh overall and fifth among the women (after Clara Bow, Gloria Swanson, Pola Negri, and Colleen Moore) in a 1926 popularity poll conducted by *Photoplay*. Bellamy would recall, "It was a wild time in Hollywood. The writers wrote wild parts for us to play, and we played these parts offscreen as well." Bellamy remembered passing through the "Mae Murray moueing (pouting) period and the Pola Negri lowering phase seen in my portraits of this period."

Bellamy's description of Hollywood in the 1920s is telling. "Hollywooders lived unreal lives, believing that activity was life, and that things brought happiness. We were tired and sleepless and weary of all the nothingness, but we ran faster and faster to catch each gold ring on the merry-go-round that grew louder and more raucous, drowning out thought."

No one ran faster than Negri herself, who admitted that the "gorgeous smiles enchanted the entire world but often hid insecurities that drove these chosen few to the excesses of depravity."

Acclaimed screenwriter and author Anita Loos (*Gentlemen Prefer Blondes)* remembered early Hollywood's sexuality permeating America. "In its heyday Hollywood reflected, if it did not actually produce, the sexual climate of our land." She remembers the ladies of the town having their pubic hair shaved like a heart or a derby hat, the emblem of the popular New York governor and presidential candidate, Al Smith.

Loos wrote in 1974, "Less and less do men need women. More and more do gentlemen prefer gentlemen."

Homosexuality was commonplace in Hollywood, although any such admission by stars would surely have ended their careers. Silent-film beauty Anita Page recalled the handsome Ramon Novarro, her close friend, who was gay. "If all my leading men had been like Ramon, I could have relaxed!"

Polish actress Dagmar Godowsky, daughter of highly regarded pianist and composer Leopold Godowsky, was another beautiful and vibrant vamp of the '20s. Some would consider Godowsky a rival or even a threat to Negri; but, in reality, Negri's appeal eclipsed hers. The persona of silent-film Hollywood is described in Godowsky's memoir:

> I hissed my way through a hundred interviews, laughing at myself and the world
> that believed such nonsense, and I adored every minute of it… I was the

"snake woman" and my skin supposedly shed every spring. I'm not exaggerating. It's all there in those early issues of *Photoplay.*

The screen was silent. Lucky for most. For who were they, the stars? With few exceptions (Negri being one), waitresses, chorus girls, girls from the farm—made overnight. Cowboys, truck drivers, clerks—suddenly suave men of the world! From rags to bitches! It was unbelievable. Daughters of washerwomen were publicly slapping French maids' faces and dragging their chinchilla in the unpaved streets. Everyone believed his own publicity, and it was written by cretins.

17. Dagmar Godowsky.

Jimmy Fidler started as an actor and found it not to his liking. After working for a spell at Paramount, he quit to be a freelance press agent, becoming an early gossip columnist and confidante to the stars. In reassessing the Hollywood of the 1920s, especially its later years, Fidler made a vivid point. "You can't put your finger on one star today who comes close to approaching the glamour of Valentino, Pola Negri, or Gloria Swanson. There was glamour attached to silent pictures, particularly. The minute the stars became talkers and started opening their mouths, glamour went out the window."

Neal Hart, grandson to silent-film cowboy actor Neal Hart, summed up the silent-film days this way to the author: "Silent films offered a stage for the viewer's imagination to participate in the plot, the characters, and the action. Modern filmmakers rarely leave much for the imagination"—an observation also made by Negri—"often resulting in a deadpan audience who shuffle from the venue not realizing their participation was effectively stolen." This, I feel, was an excellent observation of all silent films and their stars.

Perhaps Jesse Lasky, Jr., summed it up best to writer Walter Wanger: "I loved the old Hollywood, and because it's gone, something of splendor has been lost by all of us."

We have to assume that the early fan magazines were reliable sources for describing their stars to the adoring public. The majority did have respectable and credible writers.

In the March 1923 issue of *Picture Play*, writer Edwin Schallert went into detail describing the hoops he had to jump through to obtain permission to observe the shooting of *Bella Donna.* It was often reported that Negri preferred closed sets that seldom allowed anyone not directly associated with the filming. So when Schallert was allowed on the set he took careful notes as he closely observed Negri and her performance before the camera.

His description is amusing and undoubtedly accurate: "A shriek rent the air. It was the climax. The torment of music ceased, and Pola Negri, a quivering, throbbing, brooding black mound of nerves, lay huddled together upon the floor in front of the gilt doorway."

His observation was enough to make anyone stand up and take notice, particularly those fans with a rabid interest in this ever-evolving medium and its stars. This was expected and not at all surprising for this "temperamental and exotic" star, whose private life would prove as dramatic as her professional life. The public, of course, loved it. Not necessarily so for those actively involved in a production.

Howard Greer, fashion designer and long-time supporter of Negri, recalled with awe how she had driven Famous Players–Lasky to let her choose her own stories, her directors, her actors, and even what time the shooting should commence. No wonder when he was assigned to create Negri's costumes, "her dynamic personality was enough to scare the daylights out of me."

"Those who have appeared in her picture," Schallert reported, "have confessed to me their absolute inability to cope with her. They accuse her, in fact, of not *giving* a single thing. She rules the set absolutely as its mistress and that is something that can well be understood after one watches her and realizes how much of herself she literally hurls into her acting."

18. Negri with Conway Tearle; *Bella Donna.* 1923.

"When I weep," Negri told Schallert, "it is not for myself alone, it ees for everybody. I theenk always of audience, people, everywhere, all, sorrowful, weeping wiz me. I poot my whole heart, my whole soul into my art, my expression, my tears, so zat zey may feel wiz me what I feel, so zay perhaps suffair what I suffair."

26

As for her banal role in *Bella Donna*, she stated, "I do not believe she should be play'
like bad woman—like vampire—I do not believe that woman are evair vampire by nature.
Woman become vampire because of situation."

Years later Negri reiterated her unhappiness with her first American film. "The public
who had so admired my work in *DuBarry, Carmen,* and other European films was being
extraordinarily kind and tolerant in accepting *Bella Donna*."

19. *Bella Donna*, 1923. Negri with Conrad Nagel.

Negri frequently insisted that she did not "want to play ze bad ladies." Nevertheless,
she wasted no time in portraying a very temperamental one with her antics on and off
the set.

It was imperative for Negri to have music while acting. Silent films, after all, were
never silent; they relied on music, in production and when shown.

20. *A Woman of the World*, 1925. Musicians set the mood.

"In Europe she was accustomed to have only the finest sort of compositions accompany her acting," Schallert wrote in *Picture Play.* "Tchaikovsky, Beethoven, and sometimes—though rarely, because he depresses her—Wagner."

With *Bella Donna* it was no exception. When Negri arrived in Hollywood and all the jazz ensembles (this being the Roaring Twenties) were brought in, she banished them off the set. It was "only after many fits of temperament and finally an absolute refusal to work, that she finally obtained a makeshift piano and cello that pleased her," Schallert wrote.

Budd Schulberg, son of Paramount's west coast studio head B. P. Schulberg, recalled his father's reaction to Pola Negri's difficult nature on and off the set. "She was always fussing about things, he complained, and making impossible demands. I remember one night [B. P.'s] having to leave the dinner table and drive out to her because she was refusing to go to work the next morning. He went off and came back cursing her, 'that spoiled Polish bitch!' What with Negri and Swanson, there was no peace."

The importance of Negri's first major American film was huge. Paramount surely spent a great deal of money on "one of the most expensive publicity campaigns in the history of motion pictures." *Moving Picture World* reported that "thousands of columns of publicity have been printed in newspapers and magazines on the exotic Paramount star" since her arrival in America. Reports in the newspapers alone were reportedly over ten thousand columns.

Photoplay reported her salary at five thousand dollars a week and commented that Hollywood was "the land of Get-Rich-Quick Youth. Nowhere on earth at any time was youth so richly rewarded."

21. Banquet: B. P. Schulberg to the left of Negri (top right).

Meanwhile, Hollywood was infatuated with Negri but trying to figure out the artist and the woman. In a *Motion Picture Magazine* article, Harry Carr, an influential film critic who also wrote scenarios, called Negri a "she-tiger," claiming Negri had "the tiger's magnificent disdain. She walked into Hollywood with the hauteur of an empress." This hauteur was intriguing to a point but eventually would not endear her to her fans or studio.

Calling her more "bitable than kissable," Carr implied the other Hollywood actresses did not care for Negri (and they probably didn't). He reported that she ordered the studio to provide her a new dressing room and said Hollywood could "go hang" for all she cared. She flew into a rage on the sets if she was crossed in any way.

Director Raoul Walsh remembered when Charlie Eyton, one of the stockholders and producers at Paramount, came on the set during filming and chastised Negri for her continual tardiness. "She followed him off the set, shouting curses in Polish and broken English that drowned out the near-hysterics of everyone within earshot."

A star in the 1920s silent films could get away with that. Today Negri would have been dismissed almost immediately; but at that time, the public lapped it up. Times were different, and the medium of film was new.

To be fair, Negri was European, and Europeans did have a different take on everything, especially on manners and how one should be treated. Even in later years she played the great star to anyone who crossed her path. She *had* been a great star. She had won that status in Poland and Germany as a pioneer in the new art form of silent cinema, along with her mentor and director, Ernst Lubitsch. Negri never forgot that.

As Carr so eloquently described, "She demands manners and a lot of them, gallantry and hand-kissing. Pola doesn't warm up to our [American] 'Hey, you' informalities." But, acclaiming her great artistry, Carr concluded that when she began to act, "you forget all her little eccentricities of temperament."

Not every cast and crew member was frustrated with Negri's behavior on the set. In a late *Hollywood Studio* magazine interview, Peggy Lowell recalled applying for work as a film extra. Casting director Fred Datig offered Lowell the position of Negri's stand-in instead. "I didn't hesitate a moment," she said. "She was a big star before sound came in. I became her stand-in when she made *Hotel Imperial*. I shall always remember with fond affection the days I worked for Miss Negri." Being a stand-in meant many hours in front of the hot Klieg lights while they were adjusted for each scene. Then "Negri would come onto the sound stage radiant and rested and relaxed, prepared to give her best performance."

Renowned Russian-born screenwriter, author (*The Fountainhead*), and philosopher Ayn Rand idolized Negri and published many pieces on her acting style and her effect on early cinema. Rand made clear she felt Negri was perhaps the most important screen star of the silent era, with her "dark, tragic eyes, which are narrowed in a wearily derisive way, and a contemptuous smile even in the most joyful screen moments."

Actress Josephine Hutchinson was fascinated by Pola Negri. She remembered she used to "cut her classes in school" to go see a Negri picture.

Author Diane Negra summed her up quite vividly. "Negri embodied a version of New Womanhood grounded not in the girlishness of the flapper, but in a threatening adult femininity."

Perhaps film historian Lotte Eisner summed up Negri's performance artistry better than anyone. "She is the Magnani"—referring to Italian film actress Anna—"of the silent era, full of exuberant vitality. She does not act; she is scarcely an actress. Quite simply, she *exists.* She has that intangible quality called 'presence'; she is her role."

Negri was proud to recall in a 1943 *Silver Screen* interview that *she* had been "the Number One Glamour Queen, according to my studio." Negri confided that the producers encouraged her to live up to that title. "Even my maid must never see me anything less than an exotic star ... Everything had to be sensational in those days," she said.

22. Negri, Glamour Queen.

Stars were expected to set fashion trends. Negri painted her toenails red, the first to do so. Adolphe Menjou, upon seeing them for the first time, exclaimed, "My God, you are bleeding!"

Many stars soon copied the Negri style with its signature turbans, white face, and crimson lips, even darkening their hair. "I set the vogue for deadly white makeup. Soon all of the movie girls were imitating me."

Negri's Russian boots with their many jewels were copied as widely as were her hairstyle and makeup. "I invented red toenails, I invented turbans, I invented boots. I wore boots in Poland, it was so cold. So I wore them in Hollywood," she told the *New York Times* in 1970.

She took credit for having imported cinema sex too. "I was the first star who introduced sex to the screen, but it was sex in good taste." Apparently the other screen sirens of her time didn't count.

Harry Carr pointed out that when Negri first arrived in Hollywood, there was concern that the film colony would not warm up to her. She obviously could not have cared less, as she spent most of her time with her first director, George Fitzmaurice, and his wife, Ouida Bergère, and soon with Charlie Chaplin.

Publicity, however, *was* important to Negri throughout her entire silent-film career, as well as her later life. Her name would always surface in the news, as she knew how to remain a presence even after her scintillating but short career in silent cinema.

In later years Negri asserted that most of her publicity was studio-driven hype. "Our studios built us up as unapproachable gods and goddesses. We were built up as unearthly beings," she recalled. One can only imagine the looks she received when sporting a young tiger on a leash when she strolled down the boulevard. "Walking a tiger made me daring and exciting."

But one would have to be naïve to think Negri herself didn't have a hand in the goings-on. It is more than likely that Negri simply craved the attention. And she had a temperament that usually got her exactly what she wanted.

When she made 1924's *Shadows of Paris*, also with Menjou, one of the gowns was lined with rabbit fur. "This is not chinchilla!" she screamed. "I will not wear it!" She stomped off the set, delaying the film's production until an actual chinchilla fur was located.

Her producer (unidentified in an article about the incident) was supportive, even though the work stoppage was costing the studio $20,000 a day. "Temperament and fire show the great artist in you, Pola," the producer told her.

"Of course," Negri recalled years later, "it made a good story."

23. Negri in her signature turban.

Writer David Stenn pointed out that screen star Nancy Carrol, when she started receiving film roles that Clara Bow should have been given, was referred to as "the biggest bitch on the lot"—a title inherited, he said, from "talkie casualty Pola Negri."

Clara herself would recall, "I remember when I was scratchin' for a job. Pola Negri useta ride by me in her limousine like I was part of the roadbed."

Adolphe Menjou was cast in a supporting role in Negri's first American film, *Bella Donna.* He would recall Negri's temperament, saying she kept Paramount "in a constant state of jitters for five years."

When famous screenwriter and satirist Ring Lardner unexpectedly showed up on the set, Negri was livid. "R-r-re-moving him or I weel not go on weeth thees picture!" she exclaimed. When the director explained Lardner was a very important author, Negri did a turnaround. "Introdooce me, plizz. I weel eenspire heem to write a beautiful sonnet."

She was unhappy with her excessive gowns, her change of hairstyle, and her makeup. She was also unhappy with her director, George Fitzmaurice. She felt he had no understanding of how to direct an actress of her background, even though he and his wife were originally quite inseparable from Negri, at least socially.

As late as 1926, writer Jim Tully did a series of celebrity interviews and recalled that the film from the Robert Hichens novel *Bella Donna* was one of the "ghastliest pictures" Negri ever made.

Negri admitted that *Bella Donna* was not her best work. "I was bored to death with *Bella Donna* myself. It was a silly picture," she said.

Although the film's review in *Variety* was kind, it was not very enthusiastic. Calling it "a simple tale for simple people," the review stated that Negri did not register well on screen (something of an enigma, as her German films were enormously successful in Europe and America). "Her scheme for anguish appears to be a line drawn across her cheek and a drop of glycerine under the left eye. One-eyed criers are new over here."

One part of her character impressed the writer. "As a vamp in *Bella Donna*, Pola will make you forget the others … If the Famous [Players] is out to make Negri the star vamp of pictures, this feature will give her a big start."

In her autobiography, Negri said she did not want Hollywood to think of her as only capable of playing vamp roles. However, as writer Marjorie Rosen so aptly pointed out, "Hollywood, adamant about its preconceived notions, was not easily deterred from this stereotype. They had imported Negri, and she was at their mercy."

The New York release of *Bella Donna* was the week of April 15, 1923. Negri had been in America a mere eight months when the December 1923 issue of *Motion Picture Classic* stated that the film was an artistic failure, partly because "Pola began figuring out what to do instead of plunging right in when she had a director she knew and trusted."

After Harry Carr interviewed Negri for the August 1923 issue of *Motion Picture Classic*, he said the critics had been quite brutal in their appraisal of *Bella Donna*. However, he stated Negri blamed that on the Lasky management's attempts to "soften the hearts of the censors."

Negri was always concerned with censorship, especially as her earlier German films had not been under such scrutiny. Then again, this was not Europe. This was Hollywood, where scandals had rocked the motion picture industry.

In 1921, a young actress, Virginia Rappé, was allegedly raped and brutalized by America's funny man, Roscoe "Fatty" Arbuckle. Minta Durfee Arbuckle, Fatty's wife, years later said Rappé was a "small-time actress at Keystone who was so promiscuous she'd spread syphilis all over the studio." Though finally acquitted after three trials for manslaughter, Arbuckle's career never recovered. An exceptional comedian was ruined and a starlet lay dead.

Then, on February 2, 1922, Famous Players–Lasky director William Desmond Taylor was shot to death in his home. While the circumstances of his death were never solved, Mary Miles Minter and Mabel Normand had been at his residence that evening. As a result of the association, even though neither woman was charged in the death, their careers were ruined. The public was demanding more responsibility and decency from Hollywood's heroes and heroines.

Negri's future director Herbert Brenon went public in stating to the *New York Times* that the industry "is bound to suffer as a result [of the Taylor killing]. Just as it received a setback after the Arbuckle case, so it will receive another setback now, and people all over the country will regard such happenings in Hollywood as representative of the moving picture industry, which they are not."

24. Negri postcard portrait.

Scandals involving substance abuse had arisen, too. Film idol Wallace (Wally) Reid was given morphine after sustaining a head injury in a train crash while filming on location in 1919. Sadly, he became addicted and turned to heavy drinking. In 1922 he was placed in a sanitarium. He died there on January 18, 1923.

Olive Thomas was an up-and-coming film star when she married Jack Pickford, Mary's brother, in 1916. While in Paris in 1920, Thomas was hospitalized and later died, as a result of ingesting poison. Rumors in the press suggested she and Jack led wild lives of "champagne and cocaine orgies." Although her death was eventually ruled as accidental, it was one of the earliest and worst of Hollywood scandals, as many believed her death to have been a drug overdose.

Born out of all this was the Hays Code. The film industry formed the Motion Picture Producers and Distributors Association, which would regulate morality on and off the screen. Will Hays, postmaster general in President Warren G. Harding's cabinet, was chosen to spearhead the organization. In June 1922, his office issued a warning to the industry to clean up its act.

To his credit, *Photoplay* editor James R. Quirk made an impassioned plea to his readers in August 1925 to write directly to Will Hays and demand that Fatty Arbuckle be allowed to make films again. Quirk asked for mercy from the churchgoing public, who he said held on to not only the Constitution but also the teachings "of the Man of Jerusalem." Sadly, though, Arbuckle is remembered as only a villain, despite his acquittal.

Gloria Swanson's memoirs recalled that the early European films, such as those Negri and Lubitsch were making, were important because the foreign market was able to deal more explicitly with certain themes, while the Hays Code governed American films, approving or dismissing them based on their morality.

As Swanson so eloquently put it, "America was, after all, the land of flappers, bootleggers, jazz, and roadsters … As filmmakers grew aware that Europeans dealt quite explicitly with sex and decadence on the screen, and with great success, they became more and more fascinated by directors like Ernst Lubitsch and stars like Pola Negri."

Swanson may well have admired the freer sexual attitude of European cinema and Negri's prior work there. She herself was not immune to criticism by American standards of morality. She had already been married twice. She was only seventeen when she married her first husband, actor Wallace Beery; she claimed Beery raped her on their wedding night.

Then in 1922 Swanson fell in love with her married director, Mickey Neilan. "I was on slippery ground," she recalled. "Having an affair with Mickey Neilan, the most popular man in town in those days, was a bit like playing cops and robbers with loaded guns."

Negri made clear her opposition to American censorship in the April 1924 issue of *Photoplay.* "The chief handicap of screen progress in America, as I see it, is arbitrary restriction. Rules of censorship, policies, and exhibitors, all combine to limit and standardize expression. Nevertheless, we shall have variety. An artist can express himself even with the most vigorous restrictions, because he is capable of subtlety."

Negri was never subtle in her public persona, to be sure. As an actress, however, she could play *very* subtle roles. She did so in her virtuoso performance in 1924's *Forbidden Paradise*, directed by Ernst Lubitsch. Laden with sexual overtones, it could never have passed the scrutiny of the censors without Negri's immense understanding and talent—and, perhaps more so, Lubitsch's uncanny ability—to offer intense sexuality in such a veiled and appealing way.

Had Negri been given more opportunities (or, more suited to her personality, *demanded* additional opportunities) to have Lubitsch as her director, she would have undoubtedly received even greater acclaim as a silent star. They understood each other's eccentricities. There existed a natural chemistry between the two, which was absent from Lubitsch's attempt to direct America's Sweetheart, Mary Pickford, in her controversial 1923 film, *Rosita*.

Pickford disliked Lubitsch immensely. Writer Scott Eyman offers her polite, understated summation: "Lubitsch could understand Pola Negri or Gloria Swanson, but he didn't understand me."

Negri knew that the persona she had worked so hard to develop and maintain throughout her life was, quite simply, what her fans most desired and expected. The persona she displayed became Negri's own reality, much like the fictitious character of Norma Desmond in Billy Wilder's *Sunset Boulevard*.

25. Negri in chinchilla coat.

In 1970, when publicizing Negri's newly released autobiography, her publisher, Larry Ashmead, remembered:

> When she was in New York, she thought everyone knew who she was. Most people didn't, but they knew she was *somebody*. I remember how people would stare—it wasn't just the full-length chinchilla coat but the way she carried herself.
>
> She was always the star.

26. Negri on the cover of *Screenland*, July 1924.

 # THREE

THE FIGHT FOR THE CROWN

Whatever they may say about it, the fact remains: The most interesting contest in the history of the screen is the struggle for supremacy between Gloria Swanson and Pola Negri.

—*Motion Picture Magazine*, 1925

POLA NEGRI AND GLORIA SWANSON both were huge Paramount stars, close in age, each with her own devoted followers. Swanson claimed that in the fall of 1922 the studio planned to promote a feud between the two stars for publicity purposes. As they had never met, Swanson claimed there was no real rivalry, but that Negri "made hay of it." This seems likely, as Negri's penchant for any type of publicity, good or bad, was well known.

Whether the two stars hated each other or simply chose to ignore each other, one cannot assess the career of Pola Negri without examining her feud, real or not, with her American counterpart, Gloria Swanson. The myth has morphed into legend, and one is inclined to believe there was at least some truth to their bitter, if not amusing, rivalry.

None of it reportedly bothered Swanson, who had been an American film icon since 1916, when she was featured in Mack Sennett's Keystone comedies. (Remember Swanson's reference to this in her great comeback film, *Sunset Boulevard*?)

Negri, however, had to defend her position at Paramount, even if the studio itself was behind the competition with her rival. Accepting a dressing room that was inferior to Swanson's, for example, would be out of the question.

27. Gloria Swanson. Circa 1922.

Harry Carr reported in the January 1923 issue of *Motion Picture Magazine* that Jesse Lasky was escorting the studio's newly arrived star around the Vine Street studio, where "the dressing room problem lay upon their hearts like a pall." Negri was shown all the beautiful boudoir dressing rooms, hoping she would choose one like the room that star Agnes Ayres was occupying.

"And now," Negri chimed in, "let us see where the beautiful and charming Gloria Swanson dresses."

Swanson and Mary Pickford, up until then, were the only stars who had been given a bungalow on the lot. After seeing Swanson's bungalow, Negri told Lasky "so sweetly, 'This is most charming. I also will have a bungalow.'"

"Well," Carr wrote, "Pola got the bungalow."

The studio had no choice. Negri received the former Pickford bungalow, which had been used by writers after Pickford left.

Whether fiction or reality, between the studio press releases and fan magazine stories, both stars became antagonistic to one another.

Negri recalled in her autobiography that when a studio banquet for motion picture exhibitors was arranged, both stars were invited and Swanson tried to one-up Negri. "She sent word that she would not make an entrance until after I had, which would be interpreted as meaning she was the more important star. Her appearance was ruined when she appeared in *exactly* the same gown I was wearing."

Mary Anita Loos, niece to Anita Loos, recalled a tale her aunt had heard, in which both ladies' shenanigans supposedly went awry. "[Pola Negri] and Gloria Swanson were such rivals for publicity that they both wanted to be the last one to make an entrance at grand affairs. But their plans misfired at a great ball at the Hotel Ambassador; both ladies arrived so late that everyone had gone home!"

Film historian Kevin Brownlow recounts another intriguing tale. Negri wanted soft, heartrending music for an important emotional scene. The musicians on other sets were instructed to keep quiet while Negri went through her difficult scene, but "Miss Swanson hired a brass band for the day, and it struck up a rousing military march at just the crucial moment." This prank was the supposed idea of director Allan Dwan, though Negri no doubt assumed Swanson was behind it.

Then there is the famous cat story that magazines savored and Negri told with relish in her memoirs. Negri, always fascinated with the occult and even claiming a gypsy heritage, stated that on the first day of shooting *Bella Donna* "a herd of felines" was released on the set.

"It was well known that I was extremely superstitious about cats," recalled Negri. When a black cat crossed in front of her, she became terrified and refused to work that day. Claiming she had to cope with the "antics" of the publicity department, she made her readers aware that Swanson, who adored cats, had somehow sabotaged her film.

However, in an interview Swanson did in August 1923 for *Picture Play's* Helen Klumph, Swanson practically waxed poetic over her Paramount rival, even suggesting a peace treaty. "The papers have made it appear that Pola Negri and I indulged in some common row over cats at the studio. We were pictured as squabbling little vulgarians. It would have seemed more fair if they would have printed the fact that Miss Negri had been a guest at my home—that I think her little foreign ways are fascinating—her accent delightful."

Gossip queen and sometime actress Hedda Hopper remembered the cat story with a bit more bite. "Gloria's loyalists scoured back alleys, rounding up stray cats to let them loose inside the studio. Cans of milk were put out to woo them, tidbits of liver thrown hither and yon."

Harry Carr reported the cat incident in his column, stating that Negri's "grandest row up to date" was the one with Swanson over the studio cats. "Pola said she couldn't stand them yowling around and they all would have to be gotten rid of." Swanson, he asserts, claimed she would never act again if the cats were killed. "Although the cats are still there, it is claimed that they now yowl only in whispers."

Concurring that it was the idea of some press agent to dream up the fight, Hopper reported Swanson had to one-up Negri again, no doubt feeding fuel to the fire. "[Swanson] rode from her dressing room to the set in a wheel chair, like a surrey with the fringe on top, pushed by a Negro boy."

"All the females on Hollywood Boulevard were clearly divided into two camps," recalled Swanson. "The Pola Negri bunch wore white faces and red lips, and my team used no powder at all and wore a single earring, [because] I had lost an expensive earring."

28. Peggy Hopkins Joyce.

As the movie colony was taking sides, none was as public as Peggy Hopkins Joyce, who blasted Negri in an article about the best lovers of the screen, in November 1923's *Screenland*:

Most screen stars think if their lips meet for a certain length of time with a fair amount of force—that *that's* a kiss! They don't know that they have bodies and souls. Gloria Swanson does and she makes you know that she feels the kiss all through her. It isn't just acting.

That's what Pola Negri does—just acts as though she were being kissed. Isn't that silly though? Most people think she is the great screen vamp, because she's foreign and foreigners are supposed to be passionate and skilled in kissing, but Pola Negri can take lessons from Gloria all right.

The fans started to weigh in. One letter appeared in the July 1923 *Picture Play*, from a Mrs. H. A. Wier of Dallas, Texas. Clearly an admirer of Negri, Wier coyly admonished Swanson, though not by name. "I have just read … that the beautiful Pola had a mean disposition and that she wasn't getting along the best in the world with some of our actresses. The fairer sex are probably very envious of her, and I too would be, were I one of her competitors. I not only would have 'put an end' to the cats around the studio, but I would have exterminated everyone in Hollywood! Here's hoping she will lay them all in the shade."

Fan Marianne Jackson didn't hold back on letting Swanson know her feelings in a letter in August 1925's *Picture Play*. "I am disillusioned. Lillian Gish and Gloria Swanson were my favorite stars. I read where Gloria Swanson was complaining bitterly because Paramount had given Pola Negri a big farewell party. The divine Gloria answered, according to the article, that *she* was the most important star in the film industry, and how dared anyone give Pola a party! *Sic transit* Gloria from my affections."

"It's the age-old struggle between the Slav and the Scandinavian," reported *Motion Picture Magazine*. Comparing Negri (again) to a tiger and Swanson to a white bull terrier, the writer observed, "Nobody ever stopped loving a bull terrier, but nobody ever tired of looking at a tiger." In other words, both were highly admired, "destined to be the two greatest actresses the screen has ever known."

The stars appeared to have antagonized each other, although of course each one's description years later indicated the friction was the other's fault. The conflict was aided by a fiercely astute publicity department at Paramount.

"They did everything they could to promote a feud between us," recalled Swanson. Because, as Swanson recalled, Negri had "roughly the same screen image as mine," the studio insinuated that Negri planned to "put down all the other *femme fatales*—but mostly me—and take over Hollywood."

29. Swanson.

According to Negri, "Every unkind thing that was said about me was attributed to Gloria Swanson."

A. C. Lyles came to Paramount in 1928 and remembered the two stars well. "They *were* rivals, even Swanson told me that. I don't know of anything they did to harm each other's careers, but evidently at the time, it sounded like it was a good thing to do. The public picked up on it, the papers picked up on it, and the publicity department picked up on it." Lyles recalled that he wasn't sure "if it was one of those things where they wanted to do the one-upmanship on the other one."

As writers Richard Griffith and Arthur Mayer point out, the Negri-Swanson feud "perhaps consisted of little more than mutual snubs, but it was troublesome enough to cause Adolph Zukor"—the head of Paramount Famous Lasky Corporation—"to put a continent between the warring divas, the Swanson productions being transferred to Paramount's Astoria studios while Miss Negri"—or, as she preferred to be called, Madame Negri—"held forth in Hollywood."

Gloria Swanson eventually left Paramount for United Artists, where she could produce her own films.

Screenland published a July 1924 article on the two stars and how they had both changed for the better, so one must assume there had always been a noticeable dislike for each other. Negri had rejected her dressing room because Swanson had a bungalow; she had thrown out the screenwriters in Mary Pickford's old one to take it over. But now, according to the writers, she had "transformed herself to a tractable, hard-working actress." Once arrogant and condescending to everyone, "she no longer treated [her fellow workers] like something that slipped in when the door was left open."

Doing little to win affection and, in part, because she was a "stranger in a strange land," Negri stated the next time she was on the set she would "embrace ze electricians and say, 'Oh, what nice lights you make.'"

As for Swanson, she must have had "a mental face lifting." Stating that she had recovered from her clotheshorse complex and developed into a "new screen personality," *Screenland* wondered whether it also could be that her rivalry with Negri had "put the American star on her mettle."

Swanson had been accused of putting her fashion sense before her acting chops. When critics and women, especially, lauded her exotic apparel, she supposedly took notice and became concerned that this was all she had become: the American Venus with a wardrobe. No mention was made of Negri's equally extensive and glamorous trappings, certainly on par with Swanson's fashion sensibilities. Despite her keeping her meticulous dress and elaborate costumes, Swanson was no longer interested in being the screen's "greatest mannequin."

Swanson had even lost her "Glyn complex." Elinor Glyn was an aristocratic English writer who had arrived in Hollywood in 1920. Glyn took over the Lasky studio, sharing her expertise with a young Valentino, Swanson, and later Clara Bow. Swanson was enamored with Glyn, abiding her every whim. Swanson and Valentino went on to film Glyn's tepid novel *Beyond the Rocks* in 1922. Pola Negri, who had met Glyn at a party with Marion Davies at the home of William Randolph Hearst, apparently felt no need for the assistance of "Madame Glyn."

Screenland's main point was not lost on its readers. Swanson should not look upon Negri as being a menace or scourge, because Negri "was the unconscious instrument of Gloria's greatest successes." Implying that Negri was, in part, responsible for Swanson's decision to move east, the writer again pointed out that soon after Negri's arrival, she had gained a dressing room "as spacious and stellar as Miss Swanson's."

"Suppose," the article conjectured, "you were to hear that Pola Negri swept into the Lasky Hollywood studios one day, to be received and kissed on both cheeks by Gloria Swanson … would you believe it? Of course not."

Asserting that it was absurd to think "La Negri" was responsible for Gloria's departure to film in New York's Astoria studio, the article stated nonetheless, "It is in New York that she has done her greatest work to date."

Did competition with Negri for the top spot contribute to the biggest turnaround in Swanson's career?

Some did think that the so-called foreign invasion and its primary leader, Negri, were responsible for Swanson leaving Paramount to make films in New York. The *Screenland* article explained why that theory is so alluring: When "an empress of the European studios encounters a czarina of the celluloid on her native ground something unpleasant is bound to happen."

30. Negri with her mother, Eleanora Chalupec. June 30, 1926.

In addition, another article on the foreign invasion appeared in *Photoplay*, presumably the same year, which describes the mass exodus from Europe to America's film capital. "The foreigners are going through the studios with the speed of mumps through a nursery. They're not all stars. There are foreign cameramen, directors, scenarists, dress designers too, and they all bring a relative along."

That last remark was a slur, perhaps unintentional, against Negri, who was pictured. She had brought over her mother, had a Polish cook and maid, and employed Russian director Dimitri Buchowetzki along with Ernst Lubitsch. "The foreigners have come, have seen American gold, and in one or two instances have conquered the American public."

When assessing Swanson's chances for a successful return to the screen at the cusp of the talkie transition, the July 1929 *Photoplay* recalled her going off on her own, abandoning her home studio, Paramount. "She had done as she pleased there, for all her quarrel with Pola Negri, when the two ruling geniuses of the lot vied with each other for best dressing room, best pictures, best exploitation, and best money."

Swanson's competition with Negri was hardly the sole reason for her departure. Swanson was tired of Paramount, stating that she was "bitter and resentful" about Mr. Lasky and the studio, after "years of negotiating." She also claimed one reason for leaving Paramount to join United Artists was that "thousands of bright young things were lined up at the casting grille to replace me." Perhaps, then, there is a ring of truth to the rumor of her leaving because of Negri.

When Swanson left Paramount to produce her films independently, Negri expressed no regrets because it left her "the undisputed queen of the studio, a position with which I was not exactly displeased."

Hedda Hopper disagreed, writing that when Swanson left Hollywood, Negri's victory seemed empty because "Gloria still reigned as queen."

Indeed, in 1924 Swanson caused a sensation after filming *Madame Sans-Gêne* in Paris. She returned to Hollywood with a marquis for a husband and was greeted with a brass band and driven home in a motorcade.

Much later, Negri was considered by Billy Wilder for his 1950 film *Sunset Boulevard*. Maurice Zolotow recalled that Wilder, quite anxious to find the right Norma Desmond after Mary Pickford declined the role, had turned somewhat cautiously to Negri. Supposedly she threw one of her famous tantrums, refusing to be thought of as a has-been. Despite Wilder's explanation that he wanted Negri because she was a superb actress, "she was shrewd enough to see that he was capitalizing on her decline. She did not wish to be food for the vultures."

In a phone conversation about Negri, Wilder recalled, "Her accent worried me."

This also seems verified in Stephen Michael Shearer's Swanson biography. "She found the plot depressingly shocking and threw the script at him. Wilder wanted the great Erich von Stroheim for a role . . . Figuring one heavy accent was enough, he dismissed La Negri."

The role went to Gloria Swanson instead. After seeing Swanson's performance, it is impossible to picture any other actress in this now-iconic film role.

31. Swanson: *Motion Picture Magazine*, November 1923. Hal Phyfe, artist.

Wilder's decision prompted a telling account of Swanson and Negri's cool relationship by Negri's longtime friend George Schoenbrunn in a letter to the author. Upon seeing the film, Schoenbrunn asked Negri what she had thought of the performance. Her tongue-in-cheek answer sums it up: "I liked her Chaplin impersonation."

"Quite a clever answer, I thought," wrote Schoenbrunn.

Author Larry Carr recalled a 1964 television interview with Gloria Swanson and Werner Backer during the time Negri completed her last film, *The Moon-Spinners.* Asked about her long-standing feud with Negri, Swanson replied, "The gossip columns started a lot of talk, just to use up space, I suppose. Please bury this legend once and for all. I couldn't be happier that she's doing another picture. I think it's wonderful."

Swanson said that in order to end all of the foolishness, she had invited Negri to dinner, although no photographers or press were informed. Whether or not such a dinner took place we may never know.

Gilbert Denman, Negri's lawyer and longtime friend, claimed that Swanson was to pay Negri a visit before her death. This is unlikely as Negri was in ill health and Swanson was busy promoting her autobiography.

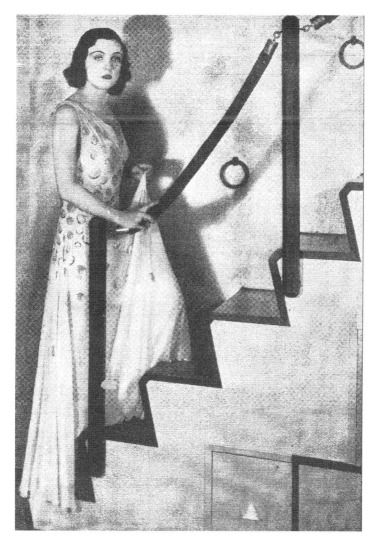

32. Negri.

We may never really know the whole truth regarding how these two great stars viewed one another. While it is most probable they respected each other's work, a deep friendship was out of the question, if for no other reason than the working-overtime of the publicity department.

As Negri asked Charlie Chaplin, "Why do they do this? I am certain Gloria does not say these terrible things."

With new fodder fed to the press weekly, Negri caved. "The publicists had so brilliantly manufactured the supposed feud between Gloria Swanson and me that we were beginning to believe it."

Helen Carlisle's blurb in April 1927's *Motion Picture Magazine* summed up the situation. "Oh! The stories of Pola and Gloria! These two women have told me, and evidently with great sincerity, that they would like to be friends. But through the Negri legend they have been set before the public as hating each other, as being jealous of each other. How now can either be the first to extend the hand of friendship?"

In a 1965 interview, journalist Mildred Whitaker asked Negri about Swanson. Negri "became every inch the star … 'We were queens of the same studio—Paramount. But never friends, dahling. We were rivals!'"

The National Guide to Motion Pictures

PHOTOPLAY

N.S.E.

March   25 cents

Pola Negri

Is Marriage a Failure in Hollywood?

Thirteen New Stars of 1924   •   •   *A vivid new serial* THE LOVE DODGER

33. Negri on the cover of *Photoplay*, March 1924.

 # FOUR

LITTLE JAZZ BOY CHARLIE

Pola Negri and Charlie Chaplin must be engaged. One may not doubt a lady's word on such a subject. Miss Negri says they are engaged.

—*Photoplay*, July 1923

INTERESTINGLY, CHARLIE CHAPLIN'S autobiography mentions Negri little, certainly downplaying any notion that the two had been lovers. Negri's ghostwritten memoirs, however, speak a great deal about the Chaplin-Negri love affair.

The historical record indicates the two were romantically involved. According to Chaplin's biographer, David Robinson, the Negri affair was the only time in his career that Chaplin allowed himself to be involved in a very public and dramatic romance while simultaneously working on a picture, in this case *A Woman of Paris.*

Chaplin's daughter Josephine, who manages the Chaplin rights and archives, was courteous to the author but maintained there were no letters "from or to Pola Negri in our archives" and that she seemed to remember seeing a Chaplin Studios press release about them "or another female." It was disappointing news that family archival material was void of the affair, and hard to believe, considering that Chaplin and Negri were in the newspapers almost weekly.

As for "another female," Chaplin's sexploits with women, especially young women, are well known and documented. He had been married first to Mildred Harris, a sixteen-year-old film extra. After divorcing her, he had married Lita Grey, also sixteen, in 1924.

Another young and beautiful vamp, Dagmar Godowsky, would recall years later, "I was so young that Charlie Chaplin fell in love with me."

That Chaplin and Negri became lovers was a natural extension of their sexual appetites. The "king of comedy" and "queen of tragedy" were practically doomed to meet and become intimate, if for no other reason than their extreme popularity and power within Hollywood's inner circle.

34. Charlie Chaplin and Pola Negri.

Negri's recollections placed their first meeting in Berlin following the premiere of *Madame DuBarry*. Chaplin supposedly tried to persuade her to come to America, where he assured her of impending success.

In actuality, they met in Europe in 1921. Chaplin had left New York in September aboard the *SS Olympic* for a continental holiday. While he was in Berlin, Negri invited Chaplin to her table. Chaplin didn't say if he accepted or what the outcome was, if he did. John Kobal recounts their first meeting in Berlin, where Chaplin called Negri "the greatest emotional actress and woman in Europe."

Moreover, Robinson's definitive biography shows Chaplin completely enamored with Negri. He found her "really beautiful" and he waxed poetic over her "jet-black hair" and "white, even teeth." Chaplin expressed regret that her wonderful coloring was not able to register on the screen, silent films almost always being in black and white. Only very rarely did color film appear during major films of this era.

Chaplin raved about her voice and how she "speaks so pretty in the German language." After Chaplin acknowledged Negri as the total center of attention, she offered him a toast with the only English she knew, "to Jazz Boy Charlie."

In December 1922, *Motion Picture Magazine*'s Harry Carr wrote that the most interesting event "that Hollywood had survived is the advent of Pola Negri." Stating Chaplin's current love interest in Peggy Hopkins Joyce, he wondered what effect "Madam Negri's arrival will have upon the somewhat mercurial Charlie Chaplin."

When *Motion Picture Magazine* interviewed Negri in January 1923 and asked the star which man she liked best on the screen, she replied, "Ah, Charlie Chaplin. He is ze great artist. And as just ze man—he is great, too. When I get to California I see him again."

Later, in a March 1924 *Photoplay* interview, Negri admitted the little English she knew at their first meeting had been squandered in one outburst. "I called him 'Little Jazz Boy Charlie.'" Chaplin, in an attempt to return her greeting, she said, mumbled in German something that came out as "I think you are a piece of cheese." Negri stated that their association in Berlin, far from romantic, "was quite casual; I admired him as a personality and as an artist."

Both stars were at several important social functions in Hollywood when they became reacquainted. By this time Negri was establishing her roots in Los Angeles, and Chaplin, already an icon, was on the prowl for another beautiful woman.

It's amusing to read their separate accounts. Negri claimed Chaplin stated his intent to see her after a minor automobile accident. Chaplin's account? Of course, it was Negri who stopped Chaplin at the Hollywood Bowl, asking why she hadn't heard from him! In actuality, Chaplin *had* been avoiding her, most likely because of their schedules and, perhaps, because of Chaplin's own hesitancy to pursue her.

They were reunited in October 1922 when both stars were appearing at the Actor's

Fund Pageant at the Hollywood Bowl. By Chaplin's account, Negri invited him to a party she was throwing at her home in Beverly Hills, where, despite the presence of many other male stars, she devoted all her attention to him. He enjoyed the attention, and the relationship started.

35. Charlie Chaplin.

After they were seen together in public, the press started a frenzy of reporting the pair's supposed engagement. As early as 1922, the *Morning Telegraph* was asking, "Is Pola Negri engaged to Charles Chaplin? When are they to be married? Neither of the parties most interested will speak for print, nor will anyone in their confidence."

When Negri refused to see him the following evening due to Chaplin's noncommittal attitude, Paramount became involved. Charlie Eyton, the manager of Paramount Studios, phoned Chaplin insisting they speak, as the situation was causing some emotional distress to Negri. One account had Negri lying prone on her settee, moaning to Chaplin, "You are cruel!" Paramount became fearful of a scandal.

According to Chaplin's account, he *was* approached by Eyton, who begged Chaplin to stop the rumor mill and marry Negri. She was ill and could not work; the publicity was bad for her career. Eyton's more pressing concern? Paramount had millions invested in Negri. Chaplin, unconcerned with safeguarding Paramount's investments, dryly told Eyton that as he owned no stock in Paramount, he saw no reason why he should marry Negri. "She never called me again," Chaplin said.

The New York Times picked up the story in November 1922 and reported that Chaplin most defiantly stated he could not say yes or no. "Any such announcement must of necessity come from her. Neither can I say no; think of the position that would place her in." Chaplin further tried to extract himself by reminding the press, "Miss Negri is a gentlewoman and a foreigner. Don't you see? She does not understand American ways in affairs of this kind. She would resent my making a statement."

But in a twist, Jesse Lasky announced on January 25, 1923, that there was nothing in Negri's contract that would prevent her from marrying Chaplin. This was no doubt calculated to protect Paramount Famous-Players, where Negri was under contract. It was not bad press for Paramount Famous-Players, either.

36. Negri and Chaplin. January 1923.

Chaplin and Negri invited the press to her Del Monte suite, as reported in the *Los Angeles Times* on January 29, 1923. Chaplin was a nervous wreck, but Negri pressed on. Yes, they would marry—when, she did not know. (Far better for the stars and the studio to acknowledge a possible marriage proposal than to have it leaked out that the two were already sleeping together.)

Both stars declared love for one another, as reported in the *Boston Globe* on March 23, 1923. So on and on it went. One week they were engaged; another week they weren't. No one was saying for sure, but each was sharing a great deal of publicity.

Despite the stars' different written versions, Negri claimed she did have feelings for Chaplin. Even though as lovers often quarrel, Negri stated that the fights "did not matter, because at least with Charlie, I felt alive."

Interestingly, this was a common observation among Chaplin's women, as well as other contemporaries. They admired his intelligence and uncanny awareness of the world around him—in short, his brilliance. Dagmar Godowsky recalled, "His brain never stopped buzzing … How stimulating Charlie was!"

Certainly life with Chaplin, even for Negri, was never boring. One account told by author Norman Zierold, is worth repeating. Negri had planned a Christmas Eve dinner in late 1922 to thank the people who had shown kindness to the new Polish actress. Chaplin stated he would be unable to attend, which infuriated Negri. When he did show up, late, he gave her a large unmounted pear-shaped diamond, stating he was too busy to have it mounted. As time went on and he noticed she still was not wearing the diamond on her hand as an engagement ring, as he had intended, he protested. Negri's answer was curt but appropriate. "When I, too, have time enough, I shall have it mounted."

Then a lovelorn Mexican admirer started stalking Chaplin. The woman even managed to get into his house and into his bed wearing his pajamas! Harry Carr recounted the story in the July 1923 *Motion Picture Magazine*, explaining that this unstable lady was outside "about to commit suicide." Her attempts to break into Chaplin's house happened so often that Negri "had a nervous collapse." The explanation the demented fan gave was that "she had fallen in love with Charley's picture."

These developments aside, one paper reported that, whether or not Negri got love out of the union with Charlie Chaplin, at least she would win millions. In actuality, both parties were making exorbitant salaries and didn't need each other's money.

But would their marriage alienate Negri's female fans? "Pola to them sums up what they all would crave to be—beautiful, famous, rich, and the wife of one of the world's most widely known men."

Then again, on January 28, 1923 (the same day the two invited the press to Del Monte), Chaplin and Negri were cornered by the press at Pebble Beach. "We are engaged," he told the waiting reporters. This was verified by Negri, though no official date was given for the nuptials.

The reason no date was given was twofold: hesitancy on the part of both parties and the fact that Famous Players had taken out a million-dollar insurance policy against Negri becoming married. No doubt Jesse Lasky wanted to ensure the success of his imported star and to protect the studio from unwarranted scandal. This was an interesting reversal from Lasky's original statement, which practically had been an invitation for the two to marry.

37. Negri and Chaplin. 1923.

Screenland in January 1923 had a somewhat telling blurb on Chaplin and his women. Among his conquests, it mentioned Edna Purviance, Florence DeShon, Clare Sheridan, May Collins, Mildred Harris, Peggy Hopkins Joyce, and now Pola Negri. It asked the most pressing question of the hour. "Will the world's greatest comic mime choose from this array a mate for his next march to the altar?"

Screen star Lillian Gish would recall that when she and friends accompanied her director, D.W. Griffith, out for a night of dancing, she'd see Charlie and his party, "which always included an attractive girl."

Negri's arrival on American shores came when young Hollywood had seen serious scandals undoing its biggest stars, most of whom were Paramount employees. No doubt, Paramount wanted no part of another tryst that would anger the moviegoing public, many of whom were now concerned about Hollywood's perceived lack of morality.

However, despite any possible worries about a sex scandal, Chaplin and Negri continued to see one another. *Variety* reported on April 5, 1923, that anyone still looking for wedding bells would have to wait "at least six months, according to reports." Negri had squashed any rumors that she and Chaplin planned to marry on April Fool's Day, so it appeared the couple "may be engaged for a long, long time."

This didn't stop Negri, according to *Variety*'s April 19 edition, from presenting Chaplin with a "beautiful painting of herself" on his thirty-fourth birthday, which fell on April 16.

Highly aware of all the press the couple was receiving, Chaplin's former wife, Mildred Harris, announced her engagement to actor Byron Munson. Harris claimed that the marriage of Chaplin and Negri was "only a publicity stunt." According to *Variety*, Chaplin chose to ignore the comment and Negri "laughed at the press statement."

With somewhat confusing timing, a huge front-page story blasted the headline: POLA NEGRI BREAKS CHAPLIN ENGAGEMENT on March 2, 1923. The *Los Angeles Examiner* stated that Negri claimed, "I consider I am too poor to marry him." The reporter, Don H. Eddy, was also handed a statement by a Lasky press agent that was almost comical. It read, "I consider I am too poor to marry Charles Chaplin. He needs to marry a wealthy woman and he should have no difficulty finding one in the United States—the richest and most beautiful country in the world. Therefore, I give Mr. Chaplin back his freedom and release him from his engagement. I wish him the best of luck and I will always be his devoted friend."

In her typical dramatic, over-the-top way, Negri further stated that now she would only live for her work and that all the happy days at Santa Barbara and Del Monte "are dead to me. It is all over." Supposedly Chaplin, who had not known of this until the reporter reached him by phone, was surprised. He mumbled, "Is that so?" and hung up. Obviously, he and Negri still were seeing one another and would continue for some time, regardless of the breaking headline.

In another twist, Negri's memoirs stated it was Chaplin who told a journalist that *he* was too poor to marry Negri. "If Mr. Chaplin felt this way, I was naturally releasing him from the engagement."

Chaplin supposedly begged her forgiveness when he read Negri's response the next day. Chaplin claimed it had only been a joke when he was misquoted by a reporter. What he really meant to say was he needed to "get some money first—finish my picture [*A Woman of Paris*]." The story, he maintained, came out in the papers "quoting me as saying I was too poor to marry."

As an aside, Chaplin *could* have been considered a pinchpenny. Dagmar Godowsky recalled, "It was difficult for Charlie to spend money."

Negri stated her studio begged her to see Chaplin, saying that she could not allow the greatest romance in Hollywood to end. Finally she gave in and agreed to see him for "just one more chance."

38. Negri breaks engagement. March 2, 1923. *Los Angeles Examiner.*

So, once again, the engagement was back on. According to Robinson, Negri told the newsmen on March 2, 1923, the day the report broke, that she was "too happy to sleep." Chaplin had relented and offered his own explanation of what it would be like to have him as a husband. "I will be a difficult husband to live with—for when I am at work I give every ounce of myself to my task."

This was true of Chaplin. Actress Virginia Cherrill, who played his blind girl in 1931's *City Lights*, recalled, "It took *two* years to complete the film! He was always improvising and changing things." But Negri was "the ideal woman," whose attributes included sympathy, understanding, and affection.

39. "Pola Negri, the New Mrs. Charlie Chaplin." 1923.

By now the moviegoing public and the reporters were no doubt getting bored with the on-again, off-again engagement. April 1923's *Motion Picture Magazine* stated it would save a lot of "brain fag" for curious spectators if Chaplin came out "with an engraved statement" that would answer such questions as: "Are Pola Negri and he married, if they haven't been married secretly, when are they going to be married in the presence of their enemies and friends?"

Negri's caretaker in the 1980s, Loretta Ellerbee, remembered her conversations with the movie star. Negri claimed Chaplin "was madly in love with her," but Negri didn't want to marry him because "he was short and silly."

Chaplin himself wondered why Negri should love him, because, as he told the paper, "I lack the physique, the physical strength that a beautiful woman admires." However, he concluded, as reported in Robinson's biography, "Perhaps it is best I do not question the gift of the gods."

Motion Picture Magazine reported in May 1923 that Chaplin's ex-wife, Mildred Harris, had been approached on the subject of Negri, whom she considered a wonderful artist. She hoped "Charlie would be very happy." But, the writer pointed out, "This is what she said when Charlie was reported engaged to all the rest of the long list."

Voicing the public's annoyance with it all, June's *Motion Picture Magazine* ran a short but pointed letter from Mary E. O'Connell of Passaic, New Jersey. It read in part: "I am not surprised to read of Pola Negri's engagement to Charles. I am only sorry. I bet she will lead him a merry dance. I feel rather strongly about the lady, but I want to tell you it is enough to make any right-minded American sit up and rave to see anyone put it over the way 'The Negri' has done."

The couple was making news until the summer of 1923. By August, the romance was most definitely over. They were spotted at an amusement park in Los Angeles, according to *Variety*, but not together. Chaplin was seen escorting actress Lenore Ulric, and Negri was with tennis star William Tilden, another rumored lover but actually a close friend of Chaplin's.

Tilden was arrested years later for having sex with an underage male; rumors of his being homosexual pervaded the media, ending his professional career and even his ability to instruct tennis. Chaplin allowed Tilden to use his own private tennis court for lessons, to help Tilden after his lengthy and arduous period of legal and financial problems.

By late 1923, the speculation of an engagement and further romance was no longer news. As Chaplin's biographer wisely acknowledged, "for the newspapers and their readers, the Chaplin-Negri romance had been a delectable farce." While the two undoubtedly saw each other socially, as would happen in Hollywood, and even remained good friends, accounts started to firm up a real end to this romantic interlude.

Grace Kingsley mentioned in November 1923's *Screenland* the house Chaplin was building. "But I wonder," Kingsley wrote, "if Charlie won't often think, when he moves into that new house and sees the touches which were inspired by Pola Negri in the building of it, of the beautiful Polish actress with whom he was at one time so madly in love."

And in December, *Motion Picture Magazine*'s Harry Carr described Chaplin's "worst-looking projection room" in Hollywood, with its one "sad looking chair, upon which I imagine the fair Pola has set many a time and oft."

The last time Negri appears to have mentioned Chaplin, at least during this period, was in an interview she did with Herbert Howe in the November 1923 *Photoplay*. She stated it is her fate "to be unhappy in love." As far as Chaplin, Negri conceded, "It end … like that," snapping her fingers. "It was a most unhappy affair; it was not the mad love that the newspapers say, not at all."

She claimed Chaplin "appealed to my mother complex… His personality interested me." This may be true, as Chaplin reportedly had a horrific childhood of hardships and poverty and even was sent to a workhouse at age seven.

The most brutal appraisal came from *Screenland* in its December 1923 issue. Alfred A. Cohn, writing a piece on the life of Chaplin, reported, "Well, let there be no drawing aside of boudoir curtains here. Let future biographers with a better command of the language of Eros attend to that. Only this tiny bit of gossip, that the dynamic Pola will not, according to present indications, ever sign her name as 'Mrs. Charles Spencer Chaplin.'"

She never did.

Actress and socialite Peggy Hopkins Joyce (married six times), who had a brief fling with Chaplin in 1922, added her two cents when Norbert Lusk interviewed her for his January 1924 *Picture Play* article. When asked about Chaplin's many "lady friends," she replied, "That's just it, there are too many (I suppose Pola Negri will stab me for that!)… He should have one, or none, because he's a genius." Asked if she thought Chaplin minded, she replied insightfully, "Not if he gets a front-page story."

Supposedly Hopkins Joyce was Chaplin's inspiration for his film *A Woman of Paris* (1923), loosely based on her romantic adventures in Europe. Robinson makes a more plausible conclusion. He suggests that it was Negri who not only served as a welcome diversion during Chaplin's filming of *A Woman of Paris,* but also, unconsciously, may have given Chaplin the "continental sophistication" needed for the film that "could not have been supplied by Peggy Hopkins Joyce—the country girl from Virginia."

Photoplay's editor James R. Quirk interviewed actress Estelle Taylor for the May 1924 edition. Like many other women, Taylor had been rumored to be engaged to Chaplin, a falsehood no doubt devised by some press agent. When asked about it, Taylor quickly pointed out that she may not act as well as Pola Negri or Edna Purviance (another Chaplin romance, in 1922), but she knew that Chaplin's idea of an engagement was "an eight-column headline on the front page." While not averse to the publicity it would provide, if it were true, she said emphatically, "I've quit taking comedians seriously."

Though Chaplin had a previous marriage to sixteen-year-old Mildred Harris in 1918, which ended in divorce two years later, his affairs with starlets were notorious. Negri was, in reality, one of many. Another sixteen-year-old beauty, Lillita MacMurray (later changed to Lita Grey to promote her film career), would marry Chaplin in 1924. Grey was cast as the dancehall girl in Chaplin's 1925 *The Gold Rush* but was replaced by Georgia Hale when she became pregnant by Chaplin. Their wedding was arranged almost immediately.

40. Chaplin with Lita Grey.

This marriage would end in a divorce more public than the Negri-Chaplin affair, with battles being lost and won in the courtroom. Lita Grey never minced words in describing Chaplin's amorous ways. "He was a human sex machine who, even in his middle thirties, could make love half a dozen times in the course of the night, and his sixth time could be as vigorous as his first."

Chaplin told Grey that Negri was "the most sensual animal he'd ever met." And even though Grey first met her romantic rival late in 1924, after Chaplin and Negri's romance had ended, Grey was reticent to meet the star because she suspected the two were still sleeping together. When Grey accused Chaplin of still having an affair with Negri, he stated the only mistress he was having an affair with was named *The Gold Rush*, which took up all his time.

Grey's uneasiness in meeting "La Negri" was more than warranted. Chaplin insisted they attend a dinner party at Ernst Lubitsch's home hosted by Lubitsch's wife, Vivian, where they were screening Negri's latest triumph, Lubitsch's 1924 hit *Forbidden Paradise*. When Grey came face to face with Negri, her worst fears and suspicions must have been realized. From the moment the Chaplins arrived at the Lubitsch home, it was Negri who "took over, even when she hadn't a word to say." Grey remembered her as being the most stunning woman she had ever met.

After cocktails were served and Negri's somewhat salty language continued ("Sharrlie, you old son of a beetch!"), Grey could see the potent effect Negri continued to have on Chaplin. "Charlie didn't seem to know there was anyone else in the room. I was miserable," Grey stated in her description of the event. Grey would have been naïve indeed not to realize Chaplin and Negri had been lovers.

Grey tried to tell Negri that she didn't like the way Negri "rasped vulgarities in a guttural voice" by mimicking the European's speech. "Tell me—how did you snare dat elusive but sharming bastard?"

Negri made no apologies. "It's joos' my vay … but I really don't geef a damn vat people sink, you understand?"

No wonder Grey was uncomfortable. For Chaplin to have insisted the two be present in the same room, especially after he and Negri *had* had an affair, was unthinkable.

Negri's flirtations were harmless, though Grey still, rightfully so, distrusted Chaplin. Knowing of his desire for beautiful women and Negri's appeal to men, Grey explained her concern. "You couldn't take your eyes off her. The contrast of jet-black hair and pure alabaster skin was electrifying. Her eyes, set very far apart, were large and dark and almond shaped, and she used her voluptuous body as if it were a weapon."

Grey found Negri's personality to be "obnoxious" but acknowledged that the film and Negri's performance in it were excellent. No doubt she felt great relief when the evening was over.

Grey recalled that because Negri was so demanding at Paramount, throwing "titanic fits of temper," Negri was referred to by executives as "the Polish Situation." Grey also remembered, "One limousine wasn't enough for [Negri]; she needed two, the second to follow the other one she rode in."

Right after, or perhaps during, Negri's affair with Chaplin, she was also involved with actor Rod La Rocque, her costar in *Forbidden Paradise*.

Valeria Belletti, a young and ambitious woman, became personal secretary to Samuel Goldwyn during these golden years of silent film. As such, she was privy to some very intimate inner workings of the stars. In wonderful letters to her close friend Irma Prina, Belletti detailed Hollywood and all the stars she knew, had met, or had firsthand information about.

One letter dated March 10, 1926, recounts a story that writer Joseph Hergesheimer had shared with Belletti about Negri, who was maintaining a suite in Del Monte. There "she entertained Chaplin privately in her apartment and [I] believe they lived for a while together there." Belletti, recalling Hergesheimer's description, told her friend of her disgust at Negri's behavior. "After her affair with Chaplin cooled off … if she didn't have the audacity to bring Rod [La Rocque] to the very same apartment—in fact in the very same bed—where she had previously had Chaplin."

Obviously *not* a fan of Negri, Belletti concluded by saying, "That is Pola for you—brazen. If I had been Rod, I would have left her then and there—but the poor fool was only a toy in her hands."

Just a little more than a year later, Negri supposedly was introduced to Rudolph Valentino at a party hosted by Marion Davies. In a *True Story* exclusive interview in April 1934, Negri recalled Chaplin's asking her at that party why she was so sad. "Haven't I been funny enough?" When Chaplin asked her to dance a mazurka and called her his "Polish beauty," Negri pondered how one could dance a mazurka "to a fox trot."

41. Chaplin-Negri caricature by John Decker. *Motion Picture Magazine*: June 1923.

According to Emily Leider's biography of Valentino, Negri saw Chaplin again, perhaps exchanging frivolities, at the premiere of Valentino's film *The Son of the Sheik* on July 8, 1926, in Los Angeles.

As late as 1928 the fan magazines were recalling Chaplin's amorous ways, when there was mention of him in December's *Motion Picture Magazine.* "At his prime Charlie was the greatest love-bait Hollywood has ever produced … In fact, his activities were so varied that even the newspapers began to lose confidence in him and now nobody can get very excited about rumors concerning Charlie."

Those words could have been applied to Negri as well. Her offscreen entanglements actually caused dislike among her former fans, so tired were they of her romances.

One, though, was about to start which would eclipse all others, making the Chaplin affair look like kid's play.

Enter The Sheik.

42. Negri on the cover of *Motion Picture Magazine*, April 1925.

# FIVE

VALENTINO:
"THE GREATEST LOVE OF MY LIFE"

> After we had dinner he stripped the petals from each blossom, strewing them over the bed. The petals were as soft as a velvet coverlet beneath our bodies, the attar perfumed the air, and together on this floral bower we rejoiced until dawn broke.
>
> —Pola Negri, *Memoirs of a Star*

"THIS IS APPARENTLY THE DAY of the exotic star. Consider the tremendous vogue, created overnight, of Pola Negri and Signor Rudolph Valentino."

Overnight?

Perhaps more so for Negri, whose successes abroad propelled her to Hollywood. But Valentino's path had been long and paved with obstacles until 1921's *The Four Horsemen of the Apocalypse* made him a full-fledged star. The film was hailed as an artistic achievement, and Valentino's tango dancing vaulted him to full star status.

Silent-film actress Priscilla Bonner recalled that when Valentino danced with a woman, "it's like making love to her, because he dances with his whole body. He was the most superb dancer I *ever* saw in my life."

Negri admitted to being mesmerized the first time she and Valentino shared the dance floor.

Novelist and playwright Michael Arlen analyzed Valentino's dancing succinctly: "He quite literally seems to seduce everybody who watches him."

In the March 1927 issue of *Motion Picture Classic*, writer Joseph Hergesheimer summed up nicely what the average American woman felt: "The average husband is a dreadful bore; he is full of aches and pains and conceit. The average wife hates his unromantic reaction to daily life. She turns to this Valentino as a panacea."

Valentino had been rumored for years to have preferred men, though there does not appear to exist any proof to substantiate these statements. His attraction to strong women, however, was well known.

Valentino's second wife, actress, designer, and producer Natacha Rambova, literally ran his career. Rambova's own affinity for strong, beautiful women with lesbian tendencies has been written about, and she was befriended by several lesbian and bisexual women, including actress Alla Nazimova and acclaimed interior decorator Elsie de Wolfe.

43. Valentino and Rambova. Their marriage would end in divorce.

One thread that seems to run through the reminiscences of Valentino was simply this: He was a genuine and sincere, nice man. His sentimental, generous, and artistic personality seemed to permeate all of his relationships, private or public.

Lillian Gish recalled Valentino as "simple, unpretentious, very much the Italian gentleman," traits echoed by Bonner. Gish marveled at his many talents, which included making riding clothes for Gish and her sister Dorothy. His two main loves were horses and dancing, but he was fond of cooking, too. As Valentino was Italian, he loved pasta, and Gish recalled he would "go into our kitchen and cook spaghetti for us."

Negri would recall his fondness for Italian cooking. She told Loretta Ellerbee that Valentino "cooked the best spaghetti in the whole world."

Leatrice Gilbert Fountain, daughter of silent stars John Gilbert and Leatrice Joy, recalled in her correspondence that on one occasion her parents were with Valentino, "driving down to Palm Springs to avoid the reviews and his possible failure before *Four Horsemen of the Apocalypse* opened in Hollywood. At the old Desert Inn, he cooked spaghetti and meatballs for them in the great empty kitchen. When the reviews came in, of course, he was a star."

Claire Windsor, however, who graced the silent screen with her beauty and later made the transition to talking films, painted a rather different picture of Valentino. She met him at the Alexandria Hotel during the time he was working on his first major breakout, *The Four Horsemen of the Apocalypse.* "He had danced me all over the floor, giving me that glance with his eyes that got everybody crazy afterward."

44. Valentino: "That glance with his eyes that made everybody crazy."

Valentino then asked to walk Windsor home. They stopped off at his hotel, and he asked her to come in to see some of his pictures from Italy. (The come-on line "would you like to see some of my etchings" springs to mind!) She claimed that the minute the naïve "green punk kid from Kansas" entered his room, Valentino "began chasing me around the room, tearing at my clothes … I pleaded with him, 'Please don't! Please take me home!'" Eventually, he relented and took her home, but "he never asked me out again."

One way or another, Valentino and Negri were destined to be linked. Author and film historian William K. Everson wisely points out that "had Paramount teamed [Valentino] with Pola Negri, they might have had their own tempestuous love duo to match Garbo and Gilbert."

Actually the two stars were scheduled to appear together in *The Spanish Cavalier*, written by June Mathis. It would have been Negri's first American film. However, Valentino and Rambova were angry with Famous Players-Lasky because he was not being given better material and higher production values as promised. Lasky had promised, for example, to make *Blood and Sand* on location in Spain; instead, it was shot in Los Angeles. In response to their complaints, Famous Players gave *The Spanish Cavalier* impressive sets and crowd scenes that would have showcased Negri and Valentino. But by then Valentino was fed up and, no doubt at the urging of his domineering wife, walked out on the production. Negri was cast in *Bella Donna* instead.

Ironically, Negri filmed the same story later, as *The Spanish Dancer*. Mary Pickford also did a version, titled *Rosita*, directed by Ernst Lubitsch. Both films were released in 1923.

Pola Negri never did work on a film with Rudolph Valentino. How, then, did these two cinema icons meet?

Their relationship started as early as 1922, when Negri was already a big star in Europe and Valentino was experiencing real success with *The Four Horsemen of the Apocalypse*.

Based on Negri's account, Valentino wanted to meet her before her arrival in the United States. He had seen her screen performance in *Madame DuBarry* when it was released in America as *Passion*, and he reportedly became fixated on Negri, even sending a short, gushing note and photo to her residence in Germany. Negri claimed Valentino considered her the greatest actress he had seen on the screen. "Tossing the little round photograph of my first American fan on a nearby table, I promptly forgot about it," she stated. "How little did I guess that 'the greatest lover of the screen' and my own heart's idol had just announced himself!"

Negri did not mention receiving Valentino's photo and note in her 1970 autobiography, but did so in a 1934 magazine interview for *True Story.* In both accounts, she claimed that Marion Davies, actress and lover of William Randolph Hearst, had insisted the two meet because Valentino "had mentioned he would like to meet me." This set Davies off on a mission to get the two together.

45. Cinematographer Alvin Wyckoff explains a camera lens to Negri on set of *Men*, 1924.

After several failed attempts, they met at a costume ball held at Davies' residence. Negri wore one of the stunning outfits from her *Forbidden Paradise* wardrobe. She had just completed that film with Rod La Rocque, with whom she was also finishing her romantic interlude.

Davies did not mention Negri once in her autobiography, let alone tell a tale of arranging the meeting of the screen's greatest lover and its greatest tragedienne. Regardless, Negri loved to tell the story, no doubt with elaborate filigree, that Davies had insisted she stay after the costume ball and meet Valentino. "Others would have laughed at us, I suppose, if they had been there. For we two, looked upon as experts in depicting passion, stood in Marion Davies' sitting room like a pair of awkward marionettes whose master had forgotten which string to pull, which line to speak next."

Negri writes that after their meeting at the Davies home, well after three in the morning, Valentino urged her to go home with him. She begged off, as she had an early morning call at the studio.

Paul Ivano was a close friend of Valentino's and former lover of actress Alla Nazimova. Ivano, born in France and a veteran of the Great War, contracted tuberculosis, and a nurse serving in the American Red Cross invited him to Palm Springs to recover. He met Valentino, and the two ended up sharing rooms for a while, until Ivano eventually found work as a cameraman in Hollywood.

Ivano's account of Negri and Valentino's first meeting, supposedly arranged by Ivano himself, is more lurid than the other versions. After the Davies party, "Rudy went home and changed out of his formal attire and into some regular clothes. He drove to Pola Negri's and rang the doorbell. He … proceeded upstairs [and] went directly to [Negri's] bedroom. Without knocking, he walked in. Pola was in bed. Rudy took his clothes off and joined her. The next morning, he said to me, 'Thanks for the introduction, Paul. She wasn't bad, wasn't bad!'"

Ivano's story is an interesting observation of two healthy, sexual beings—*if* it really occurred that way.

Raoul Walsh recalled different circumstances for their meeting. He had been assigned to direct Negri in the 1925 film, *East of Suez*. According to Walsh's memoirs, Valentino called the set to arrange a lunch with Walsh. Walsh's agent, Harry Wurtzel, had told him, "She's hot for Rudy. You'll see." So the director invited Negri along to the lunch with Valentino. "She kept chatting about this and that in her atrocious English, giving him no chance to say what was on his mind." Valentino eyeballed a frustrated Walsh for help. He was there to try to acquire one of Walsh's rare horses, not a date with La Negri.

How serious was the romantic involvement between Rudolph Valentino and Pola Negri?

Actress Priscilla Bonner remembers seeing Valentino on the set of 1924's *Peter Pan* when her close friend Virginia Brown Faire was playing Tinker Bell. Virginia's mother was also of Italian heritage, so Rudy spent a lot of time with her on the set "talking Italian, and Mrs. Brown was very fond of him."

Bonner was adamant that no romantic relationship occurred between Valentino and Negri during the time she saw him up close. "I heard the rumors about them but I do not believe them. Sometimes the studios started these things for publicity … I just happened to know something about Valentino, and I'll tell you he did *not* have a reputation of being a [woman]-chaser … Besides that, I think he was a little bit in awe of Pola Negri. I do not believe he had an affair with Pola Negri."

Quite a few members of Hollywood's inner circle saw Negri and Valentino differently.

Director Andrew L. Stone remembered how Negri had behaved when she worked with him in 1943 on his comedy, *Hi Diddle Diddle*. "A realtor had taken over Valentino's former estate, Falcon's Lair. He allowed Pola Negri to live there and I took her up there the night she moved in. I am sure they had had a love affair. No question about that. She was in tears when I drove her up to Falcon's Lair. She'd point at the stables and say, 'There's where Rudy and I kept our horses.' Or when she went in the bedroom where she and Rudy slept, she cried all over the place."

Was Negri being overdramatic? Quite possibly—but based on accounts of others, as well as events previously written about here, history records that the two *were* romantically involved for at least a portion of their association.

Negri's friend George Schoenbrunn stated he refused to discuss Valentino with her because "as she was a pathological liar, she wouldn't have told me the truth anyhow... Had she [spoken of him], it would have been another lie coming out of the mouth of the best Catholic in Christendom." The story where Pola speaks of her seduction by Valentino as he strews rose petals over her bed? Schoenbrunn said she had lifted that scenario out of one of Elinor Glyn's early novels.

46. Valentino shared Negri's exotic tastes.

Still, Negri's caretakers in later years vividly recalled her recounting Valentino's prowess as a lover and, always, those rose petals. One woman, who did not want to be identified, laughingly said, "Valentino was her main conversation! We heard the roses over and over and over. Roses in her moonlight bed. She'd always receive red roses from Rudolpho, and how they would take the red rose petals and scatter them and on and on and on ..."

Sexuality aside, perhaps it was natural Valentino and Negri would enjoy each other. Both were foreigners in the United States and spoke several languages. Their sense of artistic appreciation and intensity may have been broader than that of most Americans at the time, too.

Negri certainly made it a point to be around Valentino as often as possible. She was determined to feed the press her stories of a love affair, even an engagement. Even so, *Photoplay* complained in June 1926 that their relationship had been so elusive that there had been only one photo of the two together.

Loretta Ellerbee recalled many conversations about Valentino during Negri's later years in San Antonio. "They supposedly had plans to marry when he was so ill, you know. Who could prove her wrong? I know they had a love affair, if you can trust what she said. I know they were very much in love for a short period of time."

Yet Ellerbee agreed that Negri needed Valentino a little more than he needed Negri. "Both Valentino and Chaplin helped her to become what she was. She liked the idea of being linked with [Valentino]; let's face it, he was a much bigger star."

Paul Ivano, who described Valentino quickly changing his clothes and driving back to bed Negri after their first meeting, agreed there was a romance but said the marriage plans Negri spoke about were a "total fabrication."

Valentino stated as early as February 1926 that reports of a wedding engagement with Negri were "ridiculous," telling reporters, "Why I hardly know her."

Valentino was speaking after Negri made a surprise visit to Albuquerque, New Mexico. He was shooting on location there for *The Son of the Sheik*.

Valeria Belletti wrote on February 2, 1926: "The only dirt on the lot now is that Pola Negri today drove to Albuquerque to meet Valentino—she has an awful crush on him."

Joe Schenck, who had signed Valentino to United Artists in 1924 and cast him in *The Son of the Sheik*, was afraid of potential scandal and tried to prevent the meeting, but he was too late. In the end, no harm was done. As the year went on, Negri and Valentino would be seen together publicly at several Hollywood events, including Mae Murray's wedding and actor Richard Barthelmess's birthday party in Santa Monica.

More intriguing is a press report by silent-film beauty Eleanor Boardman, who claimed on February 5, 1926, that, indeed, a wedding was inevitable. Substantiating the rumor that Negri would wed Valentino, Boardman told the press that she had come with Negri from the Pacific coast to Albuquerque, where Negri and Valentino "planned to be married the next morning." When a wave of reporters found the two lovers, the pair supposedly retreated and postponed their marriage plans. Boardman reportedly was announcing her own wedding plans too, but she would not divulge the name of her future husband, largely because of the "experiences which Pola Negri and Valentino encountered."

Negri went so far as to state in March 1926 that she and Valentino would be married after a trial separation of four months. They had films to complete, and she was scheduled to leave for Germany. "If I feel as I do now upon my return and Rudy also feels the same, there is nothing to prevent our marriage … I take marriage very seriously. If I am ever married, I expect nothing to break the link. It shall be for all time."

Valentino must not have been terribly amused by the stories leaking to the press about his supposedly imminent nuptials. He responded on March 10 from Hollywood: "We have not even discussed marriage. We are not engaged. I do not like the word 'engaged.' It sounds too much like a contract one has to perform by a certain date."

Valentino's distaste for the legalities of marriage was understandable. His first marriage, to actress Jean Acker in 1919, did not last. He filed for divorce in 1922 after becoming involved with Natacha Rambova, and he married Rambova in Mexico nine months later. Newspapers picked up on the fact that Valentino's Mexican wedding had taken place before he had satisfied the one-year waiting period required by California law, and he was charged with bigamy. After going through a trial, he married Rambova again, legally this time, in 1923. Their relationship was tumultuous, ending in divorce in 1925. After all this, it's no wonder he tried to remain noncommittal when Pola Negri claimed to be engaged to him!

Negri's flair for publicity and her overly dramatic take on everything most likely perpetuated this idea of a wedding engagement. While Valentino's popularity was climbing, Negri's was paling; it would not hurt her career to be seen in the company of one of Hollywood's most attractive hot properties.

But Valentino continued to show no immediate desire to remarry. When cornered by the press about Negri, he would simply respond, "Ask the lady."

George Schoenbrunn remembered Negri having a special reverence for Valentino, but recalled, "A friend of Valentino's stated that their prospective marriage plan was just a publicity stunt dreamt up by her to rescue a floundering career."

In 1967 when Irving Shulman penned a controversial Valentino biography, Negri was livid. Shulman downplayed their romance, even indicating, once again, that Valentino may have preferred men to women. "It's a damn lie! I was on top of the world and so was Rudy. Why would I *pretend* to know Rudy for the publicity?"

Why indeed?

Negri would release her own autobiography in 1970, claiming she had spent years collecting material for it. "I can prove our love with telegrams, letters, and everything I have saved for forty years. This will be in my book."

Unfortunately, none of the promised material, except for a few photos, actually appeared in the Negri book. Had the other items she referred to ever existed?

47. Valentino and his controlling wife Natacha Rambova.

By Negri's account in a 1934 issue of *True Story,* Valentino left for Paris in the winter of 1925 to obtain a divorce from Rambova, "a little more than sixty days after our introduction. Much as we tried to keep it to ourselves, there were leaks in our secrecy, and Hollywood was bubbling with curiosity." Valentino and Negri had plans to meet in England for Christmas until Paramount needed her to be available for her next picture. She claimed Valentino sent her several pressing telegrams declaring his love.

Negri said he telegraphed in French: "I clasp you to my heart with all the love of which my whole being is capable, and which belongs to you entirely until death." Another telegram followed: "When you go to bed tonight, think that I love you as I have never loved in my life."

In recounting her affair in 1934, Negri claimed, "What consolation these messages brought to me! Indeed, though he has been dead seven years now, these dear words comfort me in the stillness of the night when, sleepless, I long to hear his voice, to feel the touch of his hand."

This was the only time she mentioned the telegrams. They were never inventoried when her belongings were left to various universities upon her death. Why did Negri not retain them if they meant so much to her and gave her such comfort? One has to wonder, did they really exist?

Negri claimed to have spent a considerable amount of time at Valentino's home, Falcon's Lair. According to her, one night a heavy rainstorm forced him into the home she was sharing with her mother. "One morning at the unheard of hour of seven, he rang me up from his house … which was to be our home after we were married. 'Pola, our house is going to tumble down any moment! We will have to come over to your place!' … That meant that his brother [Alberto] and his wife, Adah, and his little nephew [Jean], his servants and his fourteen dogs and six horses were going to swoop down upon my mother and me, in the early morning light."

48. Valentino, nephew Jean, sister Maria, brother Alberto. *Motion Picture Magazine*: July 1926.

This must have proved quite a sight if indeed they all strode into Negri's abode. She claimed she teased Valentino a long time about his "sliding house," to which he replied, "I tell you I could feel it sliding!" The house stayed intact thanks to the retaining wall, which saved Falcon's Lair and a panicking Valentino.

When Negri and Valentino weren't secluded in Falcon's Lair, they made good use of their being seen together at her home or in public. Negri's own memoirs show an intimate photo of Valentino at her pool, touching her leg suggestively.

49. Negri and Valentino at Mae Murray's wedding to David Mdivani. June 27, 1926.

Negri and Valentino would serve as maid of honor and best man when Mae Murray married David Mdivani on June 27.

50. Valentino, Negri, Mae Murray, David Mdivani.

A famous photo of the couple shows them dressed up for a costume ball as Spanish dancers. The event was held at the Biltmore Hotel's French Ballroom under the auspices of the Sixty Club, the film colony's exclusive dance club. As reported in the May 1926 *Photoplay*, Negri and Valentino, dressed in costumes of cloth of gold, "looked stunning." They were awarded first place, and "when they took the floor together and did a glorified tango they were a sensation."

51. Valentino and Negri dressed as Spanish dancers for The Sixty Club, Biltmore Hotel.

The August 1926 issue of *Photoplay* ran a piece by Cal York suggesting that Valentino and Negri were inseparable. "Pola and Rudy are really too cute about it. They insist on being put next to each other at dinner parties... And if my eyes don't deceive me, they hold hands under the tablecloth. At any rate, Rudy is becoming an expert at eating with his left hand."

In May 1926, actress Constance Talmadge threw a birthday bash for Richard Barthelmess at her beach house. The guest list was a who's who of Hollywood elite and included Negri and Valentino (seen snuggled together on the sand), the Talmadge girls, Mae Murray, Roscoe "Fatty" Arbuckle, and Howard Hughes, to name a few.

Silent-film star Miriam Cooper remembered Negri and her need to have a lover. "Pola without a man was like California without sunshine." After Negri had broken off her brief affair with Rod La Rocque, she was at Cooper's home when she said of Valentino: "Oh Meeriam, I haf loff." Cooper said the affair was not only a press agent's dream, but the real thing as well.

Tongues were wagging, however, about the couple and just how serious they were. The popular fan magazines relished the discussion. One in particular, *Motion Picture*, announced tongue in cheek:

> The Week's News in Hollywood
>
> Monday: Pola says 'Yes' and Rudy says 'No'
>
> Tuesday: Rudy says 'Yes' and Pola says 'No'
>
> Wednesday: Pola says 'I go to Europe'
>
> Thursday: Pola says 'I do not go to Europe'
>
> Friday: Pola has dinner with Rudy
>
> Saturday: Rudy has dinner with Pola.
>
> Sunday: A holiday.

This particular article hit the newsstands in August 1926.

Another blurb appeared about the same time in *Motion Picture Classic*, summing up what a weary public must have started to believe by then: The gentleman was not the marrying kind. "There seems to be no doubt of the fact that the heart of Pola Negri is very warm for Valentino and that he is her first choice of all men, but there is considerable doubt about the reciprocal relations. Rudy has had many admirers among those he admires, but he is apparently heart-free, which does not at all please Pola, who proves it by slapping his face occasionally."

The remark about Pola's displeasure was undoubtedly in reference to a Lady Sheila Loughborough, for whom Rudy had hosted a dinner party. Negri, who referred to Lady Sheila as "Lady X," stated that at first she had ignored the new English arrival, until "I realized that she was crazy about Rudy and had followed him to America." Negri, always very dramatic, explained, "For a while I suffered in silence, trying to be indifferent to the shameless pursuit of my lover by a leader of the English aristocracy."

Photoplay reported in June, "For months we've been fed bushels of mushy printed avowals of her love for Valentino, who now seems to have given her the air for a blonde Englishwoman."

Negri claimed that, even though Valentino held a dinner party for Lady X, the worst of it was finding all of her own photographs gone when she returned to Falcon's Lair one evening. "Immediately I thought of Lady X, and I thought I saw her sly hand in it."

But according to Negri's account, Valentino liked practical jokes. Maybe he had removed her photographs, trying to make her jealous. Not surprisingly, the two lovers made up, her pictures were put back in their places, and Negri then crowed, "The English beauty left Hollywood the very next day."

52. Valentino in *The Young Rajah*, 1922.

Valentino surely must have been perplexed, again, when a report to the press on June 29, 1926, stated that a wedding for March 1927 had been planned. The report was issued by a Leopold Brodzinski, secretary to Negri. Her mother, Eleanora Chalupec, supposedly gave "smilingly nodded confirmation." But as her own English was no better than her daughter's, perhaps Madame Chalupec didn't realize what she had verified. At any rate, the article concurred that on July 7 Negri's mother and secretary would sail for France, where Negri would join them the following March for the upcoming nuptials.

On July 8, 1926, Valentino and Negri celebrated the opening of *The Son of the Sheik* at Grauman's Chinese Theatre with Mae Murray and her new husband, David Mdivani. When the troupe proceeded to Cocoanut Grove following the festivities, Negri was in a huff over Valentino's love scenes with Vilma Banky in the film. She resented sharing him with anyone, and Banky, a beautiful Hungarian blonde, was no exception. "All day he makes love to the Hungarian," Negri reportedly complained.

The August 1926 issue of *Motion Picture Classic* reported that Negri became upset when viewing the stills of Vilma Banky and Valentino making love in *The Son of the Sheik*. "Ah," exclaimed Negri, "he make love to Vilma, but all the time he think of me!"

53. Valentino in *The Son of the Sheik*, 1926. With Vilma Banky.

Reporter Eugene V. Brewster expressed the opinion that "there is not and never has been any romance between Vilma Banky and Rudolph Valentino." This was more than likely accurate, as Banky was involved in a romance with Rod La Rocque, Negri's ex-lover. Banky married La Rocque in 1927 and remained with him until his death in 1969.

Actress Nita Naldi, a vamp in her own right who had worked with Valentino in 1922's *Blood and Sand*, remembered Valentino as standing apart because "he possessed a spiritual quality."

Negri had written that she did not particularly share Valentino's interest in communications "from the other world." Nevertheless, Negri played the Ouija board with Valentino one day, just before he traveled east to promote *The Son of the Sheik*. The Ouija board spelled out the message: "Take care of yourself, Rudy." Negri was terrified. She stated that soon afterward he convulsed in a spasm of pain. This no doubt held some concern for her when he boarded the train for New York.

Negri had come down to the Santa Fe station to see him off. "But on leaving him at the train, I could not let him go without repeating the words of the Ouija board: 'Take care of yourself, Rudy! Please, for my sake!'"

When Valentino went east to promote his film, perhaps he was gaining relief from a clinging Negri, as well. In New York, he kept busy with whirlwind social engagements, lavish parties, and nightclub outings.

Author Emily Leider observed, "If Pola Negri was on his mind he didn't show it, and made no effort to appear monogamous… An actor named Lorenzo Tucker, who later became known as 'the Black Valentino,' saw Rudy strolling on the boardwalk and discovered scratches on his cheeks and jaw. He concluded they had been inflicted by Pola Negri, but more than likely they were battle scars from his recent exhibition boxing bouts."

On Saturday night, August 14, 1926, Valentino was taken violently ill and transported to the Polyclinic Hospital on Fiftieth Street. A rumor at the time, according to Kevin Brownlow, was that the doctors were too nervous to operate on such a celebrity and were awaiting the return of the senior surgeon. However, able to delay no longer, Dr. Harold Meeker performed surgery on Sunday at four thirty in the afternoon. Acute appendicitis and perforated gastric ulcers were the culprits.

George Schoenbrunn recalled a conversation in which he felt that, for once, Negri might have been telling the truth. "Valentino was losing his hair. [He] had been given some quicksilver pills to make it re-grow, which might have started the appendix burst, and since they had no penicillin in 1926, he had to go."

George Ullman, Valentino's manager, was present with him throughout the ordeal.

Valentino was adamant about not having his brother Alberto sent for. He requested Ullman to cable Natacha Rambova about his illness. Rambova was heartened at Valentino's concern for her and hoped that perhaps reconciliation might be forthcoming.

As for Negri, Valentino requested that she also be sent a cable, informing her that he would soon be well. Negri was finishing *Hotel Imperial* in August 1926. Her work on the film was the reason she gave for not being able to leave for New York when the news broke of Valentino's surgery.

It seems strange that one who claimed their love affair was the biggest event in her life wouldn't have fled Hollywood to be with her lover under such circumstances. Negri said she would have left immediately but "I was deliberately deluded." She stated that the studio had kept her in the dark as far as the severity of Valentino's illness. "Oh, if only I had known what was being done to me! They called it common sense when it was really lying, in the name of business."

It may be more plausible that her studio was fed up with her temperament and insisted she remain until the shooting was complete.

While it is very likely Paramount needed to finish the film on time, one has to ask why her coworkers or friends in Hollywood didn't alert her to the severity of Valentino's condition, especially as the newspapers would appear with updated bulletins during his illness. According to Negri, everyone at the studio made light of her fears. "Oddly enough, no one on the set brought a paper."

What Negri chose to do is a more valid question. On August 16 a small press article stated she had been so upset over Valentino's surgery that work on her picture "was delayed for more than an hour." An hour does not appear to be much of a delay for a star who sometimes wouldn't report to the studio at all. Still, she claimed that it would be about ten days before she could reach Valentino by train, because "I am in the middle of a picture and can't get away."

Negri also claimed that she was somewhat comforted by the hospital's staff during the many times she tried calling New York. "When I was connected, a nice soothing voice at the other end assured me that there was absolutely nothing to worry about; he was in the most expert hands, to be sure, and everything was being done for his comfort and welfare." Even at Valentino's gravest state, she remained "isolated" in the studio working on *Hotel Imperial*, assured by "the voice" on the other end of the telephone (she never indicated whom she had spoken to) that she was needed more in Hollywood than in New York. After all, there was nothing to worry about.

The truth was that Valentino's condition wavered dangerously for several days.

On August 20, Valentino was considered to be over the crisis. No further bulletins would be issued unless a major turn in events occurred. Negri telegraphed Valentino that she planned to start east in a week, as soon as her picture was finished.

On August 21, another article appeared, stating that not only had Negri received an encouraging telegram "from Rudy himself," but B. P. Schulberg had agreed to let her play the lead role in *Camille*. Negri was "like a child in her enthusiasm." The article ended by stating that she was working madly to finish *Hotel Imperial* so she could be off to New York to see Valentino.

But Valentino had developed pleurisy, and peritonitis was rapidly spreading. He suddenly took a turn for the worse and slipped into a coma.

Rudolph Valentino died on Monday, August 23, 1926. He was thirty-one years old.

Negri learned of Valentino's death when a newspaper reporter called and, assuming she was the maid when she answered the phone, asked her how Miss Negri had received the news of Mr. Valentino's death. "My servants found me on the floor," Negri later said. "They thought I was dead."

54. One of many newspapers reporting on Valentino's death: Aug. 25, 1926.

Reportedly Negri's last attempt at phoning the hospital had been at four twenty-five that morning. She was unable to contact George Ullman for Valentino's latest condition, no doubt because by then his death was inevitable. Ullman himself had not slept for days and broke down at the news of Valentino's passing. Doctors ordered him to bed.

Almost immediately, Walter Wanger, producer at Paramount, wired Adolph Zukor in New York. While his chief concern was that there was a week's work left on the current Negri picture, his telegram read in part: "Pola Negri very much upset over Valentino's death and anxious to come to New York for funeral." He further dictated that Negri believed they would wait for Valentino's brother to arrive from Italy, in which case she would be able to meet him in New York.

The news of Valentino's death shocked everyone, particularly the movie colony. Almost every major director or star issued a statement.

Immediately following the announcement of his death, mobs encircled the Polyclinic Hospital, blocking traffic. Upon arrival of the police, traffic resumed; but many people attempted to gain entrance into the hospital by claiming to have been an intimate friend of Valentino's. Reportedly, his body was placed in a plain wicker basket "covered with gold cloth" and taken to the Campbell Funeral Parlor. Crowds started to swell outside of Campbell's for a possible glimpse of the film idol.

Luther (Lou) Mahoney, upon hearing of Valentino's death, sped to Falcon's Lair, not only to retrieve some of Valentino's expensive jewelry but also to remove Negri's negligees. He had the foresight to try to prevent what would no doubt be a scandal should the moviegoing public discover that Negri had been living with Valentino.

Mahoney was a former New York City policeman assigned as a bodyguard at the Ritz-Carlton Hotel when he met Valentino in 1923. The two became friends, and when Mahoney moved to California, he found work in motion pictures as a prop man and a mechanic. He had worked for Valentino and Rambova in their Whitley Heights home in Hollywood and was instrumental in helping Valentino refurbish and maintain Falcon's Lair.

Meanwhile, Negri was "prostrated in her hotel apartment" with two doctors being sent for to control "her hysterical condition." *The New York Times* stated that Negri would leave Hollywood on August 25 to attend the funeral of "her reported fiancé." With the star confined to her bed, all work on *Hotel Imperial* was suspended until her return. Looking drawn and shadowed, she spoke of her desire to have Valentino buried in Hollywood because "he spent so many happy hours, his happiest hours, here and because I am here."

Negri was seen off to New York by Marion Davies and Mr. and Mrs. Charles Eyton. Eyton, a Paramount executive, was married to Negri's actress friend Kathlyn Williams. Negri's secretary, Florence Hein, and nurse, Adelaide Valencia, accompanied her.

Part of Negri's mission was to get Valentino's brother to grant permission for a burial in Los Angeles and not in Italy. A who's who of Hollywood sent a telegram to Alberto on the ship, urging him to comply with that request. The list included Chaplin, Harry and Jack Warner, directors Clarence Brown, King Vidor, and Fred Niblo, and luminaries such as Norman Kerry, Louis B. Mayer, John Barrymore, Marion Davies, and Buster Keaton.

In anticipation of Negri's arrival in New York, crowds started to gather at Grand Central Terminal. On August 29, the day before Valentino's New York funeral, she arrived on the *Twentieth Century Limited,* dressed in deep mourning. Mr. and Mrs. Ullman met her at the station.

The *Daily Mirror* gave a vivid account of her grief when she descended from the train: "Pola, dressed in her specially designed mourning costume (costing three thousand dollars according to her press agent), emerged from her dressing room. Pola, the actress. Pola, the emotional. Pola, the Slav. Pola was everything she had been reputed, and a little bit more, for some reason best known to herself. *Pola saw the people. Pola hesitated. Pola screamed. Pola fainted.* She did it well. Why shouldn't she—this great emotional star!"

All of her fainting prompted an August 30, 1926, headline in the *Daily Mirror*: "POLA faints, faints, FAINTS." The reporter, Micheline Keating, wrote, "No acting Pola will do upon the screen will compete with the performance she gave before the mob ... of the Grand Central [Terminal]."

It was reported that she had been weeping when she arrived in New York at 11:40 a.m. She was taken to her suite at the Ambassador, where she promptly fainted in the lobby. The *Mirror* stated that it was fortunate for her that Mrs. Ullman and Negri's maid were close enough to save her. "The floors of the Ambassador, like all other floors, are hard when fallen upon."

Negri defended her actions, as recalled by writer Courtenay Wyche Beinhorn, by stating, "They do not understand me. I am a child of my race. I am Slav. I cannot help that I do not have the restraint of the Anglo-Saxon."

Her arrival at Campbell's caused considerable excitement. Crowds had again assembled, anticipating her arrival, and they charged her limousine. Rapping on the windows, the people were taking sides. Some shouted they believed her stories about her love and engagement to Valentino; others did not.

She was spirited away to a private entrance and taken to the Gold Room, where Valentino's body had been laid out on a catafalque. After kneeling in prayer for fifteen minutes, she collapsed again. When she recovered, she told reporters that yes, it was true. She had been engaged to marry Valentino.

Then she fainted again, this time in the arms of Mrs. Ullman. The *New York Times* picked up the story the following day with its headline: "Miss Negri Swoons at Valentino's Bier." After a half hour to revive the star, she was able to speak of Valentino via Mr. Ullman before being taken back to her hotel. She expressed how lovely everything had been made for Valentino in death and stated that their wedding plans had been delayed on account of their careers.

"My love for Valentino was the greatest love of my life. I loved him not as one artist might love another, but as a woman loves a man." Had she but known of the health crisis, she said, she would have arrived before his death. "He kept the seriousness of his illness from me." This may have been true, for a change.

Any further questioning from the press was thwarted when Ullman explained to reporters: "She is prostrated, she cannot see anyone. When Valentino and I left Hollywood, the last thing she said to me was, 'Be sure to bring Rudy back to me.'" Ullman neither denied nor confirmed, however, that the two had been engaged to be married.

55. Valentino's funeral mob outside Campbell's. August 1926.

New York was gripped with a kind of hysteria. As people had started gathering early that morning, the crowd swelled to an out-of-control mob that the police had to restrain.

More than one hundred people were injured in the mob outside of the funeral chapel. Mounted police had to charge the crowds to keep control. Two large plate glass windows were smashed at Campbell's, where "more than thirty thousand persons tried to get a two-second glimpse at Valentino." The rioting was considered to be without precedent in New York City. "Feet were trod on, clothes were torn, hats, umbrellas, and shoes even were wrenched from the owners."

Authors Griffith and Mayer recorded that "scenes reminiscent of the draft riots of Civil War days took place in the New York streets, only the demonstrators were exclusively females."

Author Jack Scagnetti recalled the Associated Press reporting that "flappers in gay dresses and shabbily dressed women with shawls over their heads, matrons attired in elegant frocks," all fought diligently for a place in line despite the rainy weather and unruly mob. In addition to casualties from the broken glass, a woman was injured "when she fell under the hoofs of a policeman's horse."

Ullman ordered Valentino's body to be placed inside the silver bronze coffin. "This crowd is likely to do almost anything," Ullman stated. "Some will try to touch the body; others will perhaps try to take a button from his coat—to touch his face."

On August 30, the first of Valentino's funeral services was held at St. Malachy's Roman Catholic Church on West Forty-Ninth Street. The crowds along the street had swelled to more than six thousand, with a first aid station being set up at Campbell's before the funeral procession. More than two hundred and fifty policemen were dispatched to handle the crowds along the route.

Mr. and Mrs. George Ullman accompanied Negri, who was heavily veiled. *The New York Times* reported Negri as the "chief mourner" and near collapse during the service. She had ordered a blanket of pink roses to cover the coffin. Her head was bowed, and she gave the appearance that she was about to faint several times during the service.

As only five hundred invitations were made available, the church was filled with Valentino's closest friends and a large contingency of film folk and other celebrities. Jean Acker, Valentino's first wife, was present and also collapsed during the service. Dr. Sterling Wyman was present with two attending nurses who provided a first aid station in the church's vestibule.

One account of Negri's grief was provided by M. M. Marberry thirty-nine years later. Marberry stated that she moaned so loud that her sighs were heard above the church's pipe organ. In addition, Marberry observed that the ejection of photographers from the church had a calming effect on Negri, who was less emotional in the absence of a camera.

Gloria Swanson would recall in her memoirs: "His funeral sickened me. People lined up for ten blocks to file past his corpse, and mobs of women in the street screamed and tore their hair." She remembers Negri being the center of attention and claiming to be "the only woman Valentino had ever loved."

Silent star Colleen Moore, a huge celebrity in her own right, remembered Negri as a publicity seeker. "Maybe she was [Valentino's great love], but Hollywood tended to regard her performance [at his funeral] as a publicity stunt to bolster a faltering career."

Negri's emotional scenes had been receiving plenty of notice in New York. Miriam Hopkins acknowledged that the photo of Negri weeping at the funeral "must have been carried by every newspaper in the world."

56. Mr. and Mrs. George Ullman support Negri at Valentino's funeral.

Others, however, were not favorably impressed. Writer Phyllis Leonard wrote in the November 1955 issue of *Whisper* magazine, "Pola went through her paces with a fidelity which would've done credit to Rin Tin Tin." Even Negri's fans were divided as to whether her "act" was sincere or a publicity opportunity.

Actor Ben Lyon, generally a Negri fan and supporter, said in the February 1927 *Motion Picture Magazine* that Negri had chosen him to costar in her 1924 film, *Lily of the Dust*, a boon to his career. According to Lyon, she "went out of her way to help me share her glory. That picture gave me just the boost I needed." But even Lyon was quick to register disgust because she tried to turn Valentino's New York funeral, where Lyon served as an usher, into "a premiere for Pola Negri."

Constance and Norma Talmadge had been close acquaintances of Valentino. Their mother, Margaret, sent off a telegram to her friend Anita Loos, one of early Hollywood's best screenwriters. The telegram is worth repeating here: "Sorry we weren't in New York for the big parade. I mean Valentino's funeral. I'm still wondering about Pola! That four-flushing dame—some publicity hound—they were kidding about her to Walter Wanger"—a producer at Paramount Studio—"and he said, 'She fainted all the way from Hollywood to Kansas City and then laid down on the job—but promised her press agent to come through with some really big swoons in Chicago and carry it right through to Rudy's bier in New York.'"

Even as late as September 1931, *Photoplay Magazine* was recalling her antics: "Leave it to Pola Negri—that gal hangs on to publicity like a movie mama buttonholes a casting director. Remember all the front page weeping she did after Valentino's death? Now she's picked on Andrew Mellon ..."

Mr. Mellon, the Secretary of the Treasury, was helping Negri fix her income tax problems. The press sent word they were to be married, another fabrication.

Following the funeral service, Negri met with reporters at the Hotel Ambassador and disclosed a letter given to her by Mary Pickford. Dr. Meeker, Valentino's physician, had asked Pickford, who was also one of his patients, to give the letter to Negri. It contained Rudy's last words for Negri, and Meeker felt obliged to get this to her.

"Pola—if she does not come in time, tell her I think of her." After reading this to the reporters, Negri broke down and had to be escorted to her bedroom. "This was his last message to me," she sobbed. "I must rest. You will please excuse me."

On September 2, 1926, Valentino's final journey back to Hollywood began when the *Lake Shore Limited* left Grand Central Terminal at 6:30 p.m. His brother Alberto had arrived from Italy. He would accompany the body, along with Negri, her nurse and secretary, George Ullman, and Frank Campbell.

Crowds assembled not only in New York but also along the train's journey westward. Reporters were allowed on board at various train stations and pressed Ullman as to whether or not Valentino and Negri had been engaged. Although Alberto maintained (no doubt to Negri's relief) that the couple had planned to get married, Ullman was firm in his belief that nothing of the sort had occurred. "I repeat that, although I was entirely in his confidence, he never told me so, and I never asked him." Valentino had told Ullman he had no intention of any nuptials until he had completed his career.

Riding on the train was reporter B. Jackson Berger, who wrote on September 6 that Negri planned to erect "a massive bronze statue" of Valentino in Hollywood. The price? One quarter of a million dollars. No such statue was ever erected. Years later in Hollywood a statue of a male figure called Aspiration *was* erected as a memorial to Valentino. But after repeated vandalism attempts, it was taken down.

Valentino had shot film sequences in the desert while on location for *The Son of the Sheik*. The train "slacked its speed as it rolled across the vast wastes" in memory of Rudy's work there. The westerners recalled their movie star, as small groups of farmers and ranchers strained to get a fleeting glimpse of the funeral train. In Yuma, Arizona, a lone horseman paid tribute to Valentino by rearing up his horse while lifting a broad white sombrero and bowing his head.

M. M. Marberry claimed that Negri was always ready to meet reporters at every turn, seizing any publicity opportunity. When the train stopped to take on water in Albuquerque at four in the morning, "she automatically stumbled to her feet and reeled to the back platform. There she began to weep into her handkerchief, much to the bewilderment of her audience, two drunken Indians wrapped in blankets."

And while we may never know if that scene actually played out as depicted, Berger reported from aboard the train that Negri was on the verge of a nervous breakdown. Her physician constantly had to attend to her emotional needs.

Her greatest emotional scene, Berger reported, was when she trod to Valentino's coffin, sobbing, "Ah dear boy, we will soon be home, where you were so happy and life and love were so sweet." Then, as she rose up while bowing her head over the bier, "a delicate little flower dropped from her hand to the draped casket."

Not even Hollywood was prepared for the onslaught of publicity surrounding Rudolph Valentino's illness and death. It had seen other stars die. It had seen many scandals, from Olive Thomas to Wally Reid to Fatty Arbuckle and Virginia Rappé. But Rudolph Valentino's funeral, thanks to Pola Negri, would become as iconic as the town that produced him.

It didn't help matters that Negri had a good two weeks between his death and his burial to wallow in the glare of the ever-present publicity men. The newspapers reported daily on her hysterics and tantrums. Author John Kobal acutely summarized, "Her repeated swooning from grief was mocked cruelly by the press and made her appear more a hysterical than a romantic soul in agony. Frustration with her roles meant she began to overact, on screen and, it seemed, in life."

Actress and gossip columnist Hedda Hopper recalls a very funny but pathetic tale. Writer Joseph Hergesheimer (*The Three Black Pennies, Java Head*) was staying at the Ambassador Hotel in Hollywood when Valentino's body finally arrived in California for burial. Upon seeing Negri emerge from her adjoining suite, Hergesheimer recalled that she threw back her veil to let the news cameras record her every grieving moment. When, however, one cameraman yelled that the light was not good and could Negri do it again, "Darned if she didn't! It's the only time I ever saw a retake on mourning!"

More drama ensued. Louella Parsons recounted a vivid tale of Negri and her grief. Parsons and Marion Davies were with Negri at Falcon's Lair, where "like some wild, caged jungle beast she would pace from room to room. She wept, she wailed, she clutched her long black hair, she fell on her knees crying to high heaven to let her die, too. Never in her most scenery-chewing moments as an actress did Pola stage such a performance as she put on before Marion and me."

Valentino's Hollywood funeral took place on Saturday, September 7, 1926, at the Church of the Good Shepherd in Beverly Hills. Newspaper reporters were kept very busy with stories of Negri's frequent fainting, sobbing, and screaming. "The dramatic scene of the day took place before the crypt and reached a climax in the collapse of Pola Negri, who, however, recovered herself in but a few minutes."

Negri, who was dressed in "dead black," wore a long mourning veil and was accompanied to her seat by Valentino's brother Alberto. She went up to the casket, sobbing loudly, and after kissing it many times, she collapsed again. She was helped to a divan where she quickly recovered.

Negri had ordered a blanket of red roses with a cross of lilies to cover the coffin. Many floral tributes were presented by other luminaries, including Mayor James Rolph of San Francisco, William Randolph Hearst, Marion Davies, director George Fitzmaurice, June Mathis, Jack Dempsey, Buster Keaton, Mr. and Mrs. Douglas Fairbanks, Sr., and Mr. and Mrs. Charles Eyton.

Following the service, Valentino's body was taken to the mausoleum, to a vault supplied by Valentino's close friend, screenwriter June Mathis. Mathis had believed in Valentino early on and fought to get him the role of Julio in his first major film, *The Four Horsemen of the Apocalypse.* In a 1921 interview with Louella Parsons, Valentino had praised Mathis, acknowledging, "She discovered me. Anything I have accomplished

I owe to her, to her judgment, to her advice, and to her unfailing patience and confidence in me."

Writer Eleanor Barnes depicted the emotional Negri: "Agonized shrieks of Pola Negri for the return of her lost Valentino echoed along the marble halls of Hollywood's mausoleum, as the silver bronze casket bearing the remains of 'The Sheik' were lifted into Crypt No. 1199 shortly before noon yesterday."

Reporter Eugene Coughlin wrote that the Polish star was emotionally "supreme" making her grandest gesture. "No Klieg lights to emphasize her greatest role, no audience such as she had ever known." When Negri left the mausoleum, she again collapsed and had to be carried into a waiting automobile.

Writers Elizabeth Greer and Milton Howe recalled, "After Pola Negri had done her fainting act in New York, and taken several encores, she rushed back to Hollywood, where Famous Players did their best to hustle production on *Hotel Imperial* so it might be released before the public fancy had strayed to some other topic."

In Negri's defense, actress Constance Talmadge told *Motion Picture Magazine* in December 1926, "People were cruel to Pola. I went about with Rudy and her a lot when we were all in Hollywood and he was making *The Son of the Sheik.* They adored each other. They were happy and just like two children. No one can say which of them loved the most."

Douglas Fairbanks, Jr., was only sixteen at the time but recalled "I have a feeling they were romantically involved, quite a romance, made no secret of it."

The extent to which she played up her distress, most certainly for publicity, caused Negri to become almost as hated as the dead Valentino became revered. But it would be cruel and inaccurate to imply that Negri felt no grief over Valentino's death. However bizarre her behavior or intense her need for publicity, there can be no doubt that she and Valentino had been very good friends and lovers for a time.

Negri was awash in contradiction. She clearly tried to perpetuate the story of the wedding engagement and seldom missed a chance to be photographed, hysterical in her grief. But she also went on record saying that the press was unfair and imploring them to "let me alone." Her behavior, both before and after Valentino's death, called into question the sincerity of her declaration, "My love for Valentino was the greatest love of my life," and lost her many former fans.

Nevertheless, one thing remains certain. One cannot discuss the career of either Pola Negri or Rudolph Valentino without making reference to their relationship; their engagement, which most likely was nonexistent; and his untimely death.

57. Rudolph Valentino.

Negri's version of their time spent together has served to perpetuate the mystery surrounding one of Hollywood's most talked-about romances in the Roaring Twenties.

58. Negri on the cover of *Picture Play*, July 1924.

 # SIX

ENTER TALKIES, EXIT POLA

America progresses—progress accompanied by noise. There was once an escape, into the cool, "silent" movie. Are those behind the talking picture thoroughly considering the situation? Do they know that the voice heard through Vitaphone or radio is detrimental to the nervous system? God grant that we shall still have the literally "silent" drama.

—Miss Ella E. Warren, *Motion Picture Magazine*, November 1928

"THE WHITE HOUSE IN WASHINGTON has been wired for the showing of sound pictures. President Hoover saw and heard his first talkies recently," declared *Photoplay* in 1929. If the president of the United States successfully adopted this advance in motion pictures, would all Americans follow?

The fan magazines were loaded with letters from some who feared the transition to sound pictures and some who welcomed it. By late 1927 and early 1928, as the talkie phenomenon started to sweep the country, movie theaters—at least the ones that could afford the costly expense—were forced to add sound equipment. Some studios released silent and sound versions of the same film, to appease their audiences and to accommodate the ever-decreasing number of theaters where no sound equipment had been installed, particularly in the smaller, rural areas.

When *The Jazz Singer* opened on October 6, 1927, filmgoers were delighted, as were the majority of the critics. Actors, on the other hand, were either mortified or dubious of what they perceived to be a fad.

Marion Davies, upon seeing the film and hearing Al Jolson sing, thought, "No. This can't be. There can't be talkies. I'm ruined. I'm wrecked."

Dagmar Godowsky said, "The public made stars out of nobodies and placed them high in the sky where they twinkled hysterically. But then came the Dawn. Talkies! *Finished!* The night was sweet while it lasted."

59. Negri caricature by H. Barndollar. *Theatre Magazine*, November 1927.

Interestingly but not surprisingly, Negri downplayed the issue of sound films in her autobiography, not once mentioning the crushing impact of *The Jazz Singer.* Her response, according to celebrated film critic and historian Alexander Walker: "Eet is all foolishness. Eet is a fad, a curiosity. I do not think of it at all. Bah!"

Negri was not the only movie star or director who thought talkies would pass.

Director Andrew L. Stone, whose remarkable career endured from the silent era through the 1970s, remembered the havoc caused by the introduction of sound and the outright denial some people held onto. "There were a lot of people before talking pictures that would say, 'They'll never last!' I thought these people were idiots who said silent pictures were better. You'd be surprised in the late '20s, the people who said talkies wouldn't last, that they were just a fad. It was obvious! How could talkies compare with silent pictures where you had titles all the way through? It was ridiculous."

To understand Negri's (and many others') resistance, one has to first look at sound films in their infancy, when many considered them merely a novelty. Experiments with sound recording had begun as early as the mid to late 1890s. Thomas Edison, the inventor of the phonograph, was driven to merge sight and sound. Experiments were also being done overseas, specifically by French film director Alice Guy-Blaché.

Historian Scott Eyman explained, "From the beginning, the cinema abhorred silence; the cinema needed some sort of sound, if only to cover up the distracting noises of the projector and the shuffling of the audience." This, of course, is where live music came into play in theaters, be it an upright piano banging out a melodious accompaniment, an organist, or, in larger cities later on, full orchestras. As silent films became more popular, naturally more musicians were employed to accompany them.

When sound films became a reality, however, many theater musicians were driven out of a job. The 1931 Monthly Labor Review of the U. S. Bureau of Labor Statistics was telling. Because of the rapid growth in sound pictures, 9,885 musicians, or about fifty percent of the musicians employed in theaters, were displaced.

Such startling figures seem corroborated by the records of the American Federation of Musicians Local 802, the organization of musicians in New York City. There were 3,300 musicians employed in New York City movie theaters in 1928. By contrast, only 1,500 musicians were employed in 1931, "showing a loss of 1,700 or nearly fifty-three percent of that total number."

Silent-film theater organist Gaylord Carter recalled the transition and how it affected him and other theater musicians. "The turnover from silent to sound was a wrenching experience for everyone in the industry—it just burst on us like a bomb. As soon as they could, the theaters let the orchestras go. And the organists fared little better. The *Los Angeles Times* ran a headline that read: 'SOUND PICTURES DRIVE ORGANISTS FROM THEATERS; MANAGERS REJOICE.'"

Despite many people's belief that 1927's *The Jazz Singer* was the first sound film, there were many earlier trials. The Warner brothers, Sam, Harry, Jack, and Albert, had been involved in films since 1903. After establishing Warner Brothers Pictures, Inc., in 1923, they teamed up with Vitaphone and the Western Electric and Bell Telephone Laboratories to produce the first full-scale sound film in 1926. *Don Juan*, starred John Barrymore along with a myriad of musical and operatic artists. It had no dialogue, but it did have a full musical score and sound effects. *The Jazz Singer* boasted the first synchronized dialogue, as well as the big draw of Al Jolson's singing.

Films with only music and effects became known as "sound" films, and those with spoken dialogue were labeled "talkies." As Brownlow and Eyman explain, trade papers started sarcastically referring to silent films with limited talking sequences (such as *The Jazz Singer*) as "goat gland pictures." According to Eyman, around 1920 goat testes were surgically implanted into humans as a cure for impotence. Hence, goat gland pictures were silent movies that "filmmakers attempted to rejuvenate by surgically grafting dialogue onto them."

The New York premiere of *Don Juan* on August 6, 1926, was preceded by films that showcased the talents of the New York Philharmonic, opera singers Marion Talley and Giovanni Martinelli, and violinist Efrem Zimbalist. "With closed eyes one could easily believe that the actual orchestra was playing," gushed *Musical Courier.*

Hollywood's new movie censor, Will Hays, greeted the film's audience onscreen with synchronized images and speech. These achievements shocked and delighted a curious audience.

60. Negri and her dog.

New York Times critic Mordaunt Hall was laudatory: "A marvelous device known as the Vitaphone, which synchronizes sound with motion pictures, stirred a distinguished audience in Warner's Theatre to unusual enthusiasm at its initial presentation last Thursday evening." Hall, never prone to hyperbole, was very much impressed and used such adjectives as *uncanny, thrilling, ambitious*, and *boundless* to describe the future of films with sound.

Synchronizing music to the image on the screen, Vitaphone's early impact was impressive, but many thought the technology would serve a limited purpose and draw small audiences. *Motion Picture Magazine*'s Elizabeth Greer reported in 1926, following the success of *Don Juan*, that the Vitaphone would have an important effect on pictures, but that its purpose was "not to introduce talking movies" but rather to "serve exhibitors and audiences in small towns where the capacity of the theater will not permit a large, expensive orchestra." What she couldn't have foreseen was the huge change Vitaphone would signal as it morphed into larger, more elaborate sound experiments.

"Warners did not want dialogue, any more than supporters of silent film [did]," according to Brownlow. "Their mission was to bring the marvels of symphonic orchestras to the tiniest hamlet in the land. They thought the odd Vitaphone short could satisfy the desire for dialogue. But they reckoned without radio, which had been increasing the public's affection for dialogue for several years. [People] had become addicted to it almost as much as to the moving picture."

Hollywood got its first look at *Don Juan* on October 27, 1926, when it opened at Grauman's Egyptian Theatre in Los Angeles. Among those attending were Negri, Barrymore, Chaplin, Garbo, Harold Lloyd, Victor Fleming, and many other celebrities.

Negri's reaction remains unrecorded, but she had to have realized that if sound films were becoming a reality her days were numbered. Her accent would be a hindrance, as so many foreign stars would find.

It is almost certain Negri never would have consented to a voice test, even if Paramount had insisted. Her ego, temperament, and pride would have made the request the ultimate insult. She had proved her merit. She was a fine actress—a star. And besides, talkies were not going to last.

Why, one wonders, did Negri not recognize that talkies had indeed arrived and attempt to lose her accent? Was it laziness, apathy, boredom? Even Gloria Swanson, Negri's rival from the silent days, swallowed her pride and brought American stage actress Laura Hope Crews (Aunt Pittypat in *Gone with the Wind*) to Hollywood to help her with her vocal style.

Perhaps Negri would have fared better had she been guided through the process as Greta Garbo was. MGM Studios knew they had a huge financial stake in Garbo, and they took the time to prepare and promote her. If Garbo had failed as a talkie actress, it would have been interesting to see how her devoted public would have responded. But she sailed into sound with a brilliant success in MGM's 1930 film, *Anna Christie.*

61. Negri portrait, circa 1930.

How ironic that in a 1984 interview for *San Antonio Express-News*, Negri claimed that when silent went to sound "very few survived. Do you know who passed the transition with flying colors? Greta Garbo and myself."

As 1926 stretched into 1927, Pola Negri still had a year to go on her Paramount contract. By then the majority of films were at least part sound, and the notion that talkies were a gimmick evaporated with the premiere of *The Jazz Singer* in 1927.

So, why did Negri never make a talkie under her Paramount contract, when it was obvious that sound films were inevitable? Was her vocal ability so uncertain that Paramount would let one of its former megastars leave to face an unpredictable future?

Negri still had to fulfill her Paramount contract through February 1928. Her latest film, *The Woman on Trial*, was due for release October 29. She appeared to be on safe ground with no threat yet of a talking film.

Variety reported on October 12, 1927, that Negri was in negotiations with Paramount for a four-picture deal and that she was currently receiving $8,000 a week. "Paramount is satisfied with the sales of the Negri pictures and considering raising her salary to ten thousand dollars a week." *Moving Picture World* reported on December 3, 1927, the tentative offer was $125,000 per film for a maximum of three films per year.

Already, however, there had been rumblings in the film world about Negri's box office draw and its receipts, which is where the rubber meets the road. *Variety* reported on January 5, 1927, that in Portland, Oregon, *Hotel Imperial*, Negri's latest, "did not fare so well at the Majestic—Pola Negri not considered much of a draw locally." Her popularity was on the wane.

62. Negri in *Three Sinners.* 1928.

Negri, who always had appeared a favorite in the movie magazine polls of leading motion picture stars, no longer registered. *Motion Picture Magazine*'s November 1928 advertisement for "twenty-four sepia finish pictures of your favorites for just One Dollar" featured the younger contenders, such as Louise Brooks, Anita Page, Nancy Carroll, Alice White, Lina Basquette, and Loretta Young. Negri, Swanson, Fairbanks, and Pickford were not even mentioned.

Negri's persona didn't fit the trend of "collegiate" pictures. The Pola Negri who had once set Hollywood fashion was becoming obsolete.

German author Paul Werner suggested the changing times hindered Negri. "Her erotic type had become passé, and she was burdened with a ghastly accent. Negri, as the permanent vamp, soon appeared a parody of herself."

Negri was even lampooned in 1928's *The Patsy,* directed by King Vidor. This film featured Marion Davies performing "hilariously accurate parodies of Mae Murray, Lillian Gish, and Pola Negri," according to Brownlow.

Werner added, "As far as the American public went, [Negri] was better known than liked, more infamous than famous. Her interminable affairs and scandals caused growing anger among women's clubs and other moralistic majorities or minorities."

Her popularity had suffered from her "grief-stricken hullabaloo at the death and funeral of Valentino. Even her sturdiest admirers thought it bad taste and didn't scruple about telling her so, with gestures," reported *Photoplay*'s Leonard Hall in December 1928.

Writer Emily Wortis Leider acknowledged Negri's popularity had plummeted after her "emotional displays at Valentino's crypt."

Negri sued the estate of Rudolph Valentino in January 1927 to recover $15,000 she had loaned him in February 1926. The resulting news reports certainly did not make her look like the grief-stricken, lovelorn, and lonely woman she had tried to portray.

Letters bashing Negri began appearing in movie magazines. The fans were tired of her publicity ploys.

Fans were further unsettled when, almost immediately after Valentino's untimely death, Negri married Serge Mdivani on May 14, 1927. After having expressed her undying love for Valentino, she now claimed that Mdivani was "the greatest love" of her life. She was quoted in a press release, "I did love my [first] husband, Count Domski. I adored Valentino. I became very fond of Mr. Chaplin, but Serge means more than all to me."

Hollywood gossip queen Louella Parsons possibly thought she was coming to the aid of Negri regarding the upcoming Mdivani marriage in a series of articles regarding Negri's grating betrayal of Valentino. What comes across is rather a tongue-in-cheek "shame on you." Parsons began her report by stating the world may think of Negri "as a cold, sophisticated woman who plays with the affections of men as a cat toys with a mouse."

In the April 20, 1927, *Los Angeles Examiner*, Parsons wrote, "There is no doubt that this first word of Pola's approaching marriage will come as a surprise to Hollywood." Parsons tried to win over her readers, claiming Mdivani and his brother David had been Negri's childhood friends. Prince Mdivani "has known his bride-to-be since they were children, and he has been in love with her since she wore pinafores, he told me."

However, in no other materials, including her ghostwritten autobiography, did Negri indicate she had ever met Serge Mdivani before the day the brothers showed up at her beach house to go swimming.

63. Paris wedding of Pola Negri and Georgian prince Serge Mdivani. May 14, 1927.

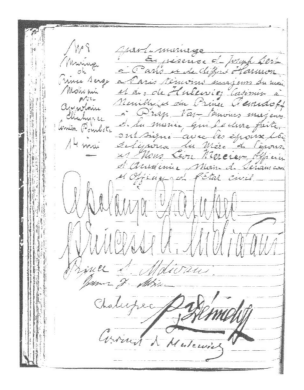

64. Marriage registry.

65. Negri signs the marriage registry.

According to Parsons, when Mdivani heard of Negri's extreme grief at Valentino's passing, he called on Negri to pay his respects and "to sympathize with his old friend in her loss." Eventually, Parsons went on, their friendship turned into love.

Negri reported in her book, however, that she thought it odd that the Mdivani brothers had "not sent one word of condolence when Rudy died." No wonder the public was confused and perhaps frustrated with Negri's contradictory behavior, falsehoods, and outbursts.

The Mdivani siblings, five of them, originated from the country of Georgia and claimed to be princes and princesses. Their genealogy is still debated, though they apparently had a minor noble lineage.

Rumors and articles swirled around the "royal" couple, prompting editor James Quirk to publicly discredit Mdivani of any royal status and chastise Negri, in the July 1927 issue of *Photoplay*: "Isn't it about time someone called Pola Negri's attention to the possibility of living her emotional life in private instead of in a shop window?"

Quirk stated that *Photoplay* had asked a noted Slavonic genealogist to investigate the Mdivanis claim to royalty, which the researcher debunked. Citing America's "natural weakness" for royalty, Quirk's report concluded, "The name is Mdivani, Mdivanov being the Russified form. It does not figure in the list of princely families of Georgian (Caucasian) derivation which was sanctioned by the Government in 1850 and which is given in Dolgorukov's *Russian Genealogy*. A lady who is half-Georgian and a native of Tiflis says that they are common gentry and do not belong to the titled nobility."

Of course, these developments were good press. Negri's rival Gloria Swanson had recently married Henri, Marquis de la Falaise de la Coudraye in 1925 when filming in Paris. Which of the two royals ranked higher?

Loretta Ellerbee remembered Negri's so-called prince. "The royalty she married into was from some defunct principality over in Europe. It didn't really amount to much. It was all bravado and title but not a whole lot of money."

Negri acknowledged in her memoirs that her betrayal of Valentino and marriage to Mdivani added fuel to the fire of fan disenchantment. "My fan mail … fell off to a series of abusive letters. The American Valentino cult was determined to ruin me for daring to live a life that was not completely dedicated to the memory of Rudy."

Negri's observation was validated by a letter from filmgoer Frances Smith, published in *Picture Play*, September 1928. "A few words of praise for Malcolm H. Oettinger, for his frank and subtle interview with Pola Negri, in a recent issue. I was not only surprised, but pleased, that he dared risk her anger. So seldom is the truth told in interviews—and I suppose there are usually good reasons, too! But this time I suspect we got the truth—and it was a relief not to read the usual nonsense. Instead, the grand and mysterious Pola failed to rake in another victim! Since her recent marriage to a prince, Pola has lost many admirers and has not gained what she thought she would. As an individual I detest Pola. As an actress I admire her. My admiration for her ability to act has somewhat cooled since her public weeping over Valentino, for it was quite apparent that her sorrow was not sincere."

66. Negri and Mdivani.

One fan in July 1928's *Picture Play* stated that an article about the "fiery" Negri was inane. "The last time I saw Pola Negri in *The Woman on Trial*, she was far from fiery. In fact, she did a poor imitation of Lillian Gish. Pola is sunk too deep in sables and luxury to have much fire left."

Not only were fans turning against her, but the film magazines and the industry's bible, *Variety*, started to point out severe Negri deficiencies, too. On March 2, *Variety* reported low grosses in Washington, D. C., stating that "filmgoers appear to be a bit Negri-shy," and again, in the March 9 issue, reported that the film "flopped at the Century in Baltimore. Pola Negri simply no draw here."

Variety reported on August 22 that Negri's name was not even used in St. Louis, where *Loves of an Actress* was being shown. "The extent to which Pola Negri is 'washed up' as far as St. Louis motion picture managers and public are concerned was forcibly demonstrated in the advance showings at the Missouri Theatre; not once was Negri's name visible." And again on August 29, *Variety* reported that the film was "entertaining despite Pola Negri, whose name has been withheld from all local copy because of her poor box office draw."

Another disparaging report appeared in *Variety* on October 3 regarding *Loves of an Actress* in Toronto. "Pola Negri complete flop here now. Her last three pictures knocked houses in which they were shown below average."

Herbert Cruikshank reported in the October 1928 issue of *Motion Picture Magazine,* "Now it seems Pola is through. Here, at any rate."

Author Stephen Michael Shearer concluded, "By 1928 movie exhibitors were pleading for no more Negri films. When talkies arrived, Negri, who spoke with a heavy accent, was dead in the water in America."

Clearly Paramount was aware of this trend. They had to honor her contract through 1928 but also cut their losses.

Perhaps, with a new prince for a husband, Negri thought she would become popular once more and remain at Paramount. This was not the case. Paramount chose not to renew Negri's contract after her last 1928 film, *The Woman from Moscow.* Although part sound, it did not treat the audience to one spoken word from Negri.

In 1929, January's *Motion Picture Magazine* gave an honest appraisal of what really had happened. "Pola Negri was good box office as long as the publicity department flooded the land with tales of her temperamentality, gags accentuating the bizarre in her make-up, nifties [jokes] regarding her charities … When they quit making nifties on Negri, her pictures became film-salesmen's nightmares."

The October 1929 *Picture Play* featured a thoughtful, if somewhat premature, article on foreign actors and their demise as talkies were evolving. According to Myrtle Gebhart, some of the greatest of stars from abroad "have returned to their native lands, defeated by the microphone." While she correctly observed Negri and Lubitsch brought sophistication and a freer "emotional expression," she pointed out that Negri was a victim of "mediocre stories," and that "overacting in personal matters clubbed her."

No doubt a slam to Negri's quick betrayal of Valentino, Gebhart asserted, "Pola with her prestige arrived. Pola plus a prince, but minus her prestige, left. Poor Pola!"

Leonard Hall's article in the December 1928 *Photoplay*, "The Passing of Pola," summed up her career at that stage. "A public wearied to the snoring point by press reports of her loves and longings didn't even snort in its sleep at her marriage to one of the Mdivani boys.

Negri, alarmed and wistful, was swept along on a swift ebb tide out to American oblivion."

Moreover, Hall made some very valid points as to why Negri was a Hollywood fatality in 1928, when she should have been at the peak of her powers. According to Hall, "she was oversold." Citing her fiery personality as a plus, he wrote that Hollywood had presented a tamer and more Americanized version than her original German import. He detested *Bella Donna*, her first American film. "We expected a tigress—we got a placid, poised, and beribboned Persian house cat, all coat and no claws."

Ghostwriter Alfred Allan Lewis agreed. "Hollywood ruined her by not taking advantage of her greatest asset in the classic UFA Lubitsch films. Pola had the earthiness of an Anna Magnani"—not the first time this comparison was made—"and Paramount turned her into just another Hollywood glamour-puss."

Hall pointed out the inadequacies Negri brought upon herself. For instance, Paramount was not about to grant her ten thousand dollars per film, but offering her eight thousand was "right smart money for a—shall we say—difficult star whose American drawing power had shifted to the wrong side of the decimal point."

A newspaper report on July 13, 1928, stated that Negri's contract with "Paramount Famous Lasky expired several weeks ago and will not be renewed." Another blurb in August stated that Negri was returning to Germany to make films. Her glorious silent days at Paramount were over.

Negri would spend the next three years almost exclusively in Europe. For the remainder of 1928 and most of 1929, Negri lived in Paris with Serge Mdivani at the Château de Séraincourt.

67. Château de Séraincourt outside Paris: Mdivani and Negri's residence.

68. Negri and Serge Mdivani. 1927.

It was reported in March 1929 that she had broken a film contract in France with director Gaston Ravel for a film titled *Le collier de la reine* (*The Queen's Necklace*), based on the novel by Alexandre Dumas père. *The Queen's Necklace* was successfully filmed in France, sans Negri.

One report in March 1929 stated she was unhappy with Ravel's project because the scenario had been changed and scenes had been cut after her approval. A report in May said Negri objected "because the producers failed to provide bathing facilities for her use." She was returning to UFA in Germany, after paying $20,000 in damages, because "there are bath tubs" in Germany!

An even stranger press report came out May 5, 1929, stating that Europe was to use Negri in a "U. S. Talkie War." An "Anglo-German" company supposedly was going to use Negri to help break into the American talkie field. "The German talkie already pooled, will thus be used to fight the American domination of sound and talkie films and apparatus." The proposed project was a film called *The Shanghai Gesture*, which never happened with Negri. It was eventually made in 1941, starring Gene Tierney and directed by Josef von Sternberg, who had brought a young Marlene Dietrich to acclaim with his brilliant *The Blue Angel*.

Negri's return to films had to wait, as she was now divorcing Mdivani. Rumors of marital discord had been circulating in the press for months.

In a news dispatch dated June 8, 1929, Negri stated, "Oh, but I am ill and can discuss nothing today." She had pulled that ploy throughout her silent-film days when she didn't feel like shooting, a tactic Swanson would jokingly use during their Paramount days: "Ah … cannot work today; must go to doctor, am seeck."

One newspaper report in July 1928 stated Negri and Mdivani "were contemplating a separation." "A friendly divorce with no hard feelings" was being worked out, according to Mdivani. He stated that the trouble was "incompatibility of temperament." This explanation was given while "seated in a cream-colored Rolls-Royce" in Paris, where he had just arrived from Cannes.

"Being a princess is not so much fun as I thought it would be," Negri told the press in November 1929. Stating that perhaps Mdivani thought that movies "mean too much to me," she said she would rather be a "film slave" than any other. Of course, she gave little or no credence to reports that Mdivani had started an affair with opera singer Mary McCormick, who planned to marry him after the divorce.

In December, the couple was reportedly "in seclusion after reconciliation" to "test happiness." Meanwhile, there were press reports that Negri was engaged to composer Rudolph Friml but "neither felt free to discuss it" as her divorce had not been finalized!

So bizarre were the continuous twists that humorist Will Rogers felt compelled to comment in December 1929. Referring to Negri's impending divorce from Mdivani and his liaison with McCormick, Rogers quipped that Mdivani "was supposed to be 'Prince of Georgia,' so I suppose his mother was Empress of Atlanta and his father King of Coca-Cola."

Negri was sued for $68,680 in back taxes for 1924, '25, and '26, not the first time she had run afoul of the government. There doesn't appear to be any documentation of her reaction to her tax problems.

In all of this confusion she managed to make a British film called *The Way of Lost Souls*, directed by Paul Czinner. It was released in the United Kingdom as a silent film in May 1929 and then re-released May 1, 1930, as a sound film with musical score and sound effects but no talking.

Contemporary film critic Jay Weissberg in his 2005 review claimed that the "dreadful" musical score by Fred Elizalde was added only because "producers feared that no one would go see a film in 1929 unless it could boast some kind of sound." This is very likely true, as now talkies were almost completely dominant. Still, Weissberg praised Negri's acting and Czinner's directing, calling the film "an extraordinary British silent."

A divorce was granted to Negri and Mdivani in Paris on April 2, 1931, as reported in the *New York World-Telegram*. "A woman's place is in the home and Pola did not seem to know it," Mdivani told the press. Negri's rationale, using the same phrasing as Mdivani, was "incompatibility of temperaments." She was quoted as saying, "An actress is really married first to her art, and there is no divorce from that."

Once Mdivani heard the divorce had been finalized, he made immediate plans to wed McCormick. "This is very good news. Now Miss McCormick and I are enabled to consummate our romance." Their romance would also end in divorce. Serge Mdivani remarried and then tragically was killed in a polo accident in 1936.

69. Negri, after Serge Mdivani's death. 1936.

With her typical never-ending flair for publicity, Negri was getting plenty of press. But readers and former fans were now uninterested and even angered with Negri and her drawn-out personal life. The United States was well into the Depression, and thousands of people had no work, no hope, and no future. While the movies did indeed offer a welcome escape of sorts, the problems of Pola Negri seemed insignificant to anyone simply trying to survive in a world economy gone south.

One has to ponder whether the moviegoing public of the time could have embraced Negri in the roles for which she had been famous. How would a countess or queen be relatable to an audience experiencing a worldwide depression with breadlines around every corner? As Herbert Cruikshank remarked, the "characterizations with which she became identified have ceased to find favor with the fans." The public now found stories of everyday men and women more to their taste than grand-scale dramas.

Movie audiences of the thirties were offered a new dimension in entertainment by the rise of talking films, as Hollywood ushered in a constellation of new stars with vocal ability. Scores of trained New York stage actors invaded Hollywood, because they had the vocal technique and projection skills that silent players had never had to worry about. A new Hollywood emerged, a Hollywood governed by the microphone and the new technology of sound.

Like live theater musicians, many a silent-film icon was displaced in the process. Once-promising stars Walter Byron, Ivan Lebedeff, Delia Magana, Barry Norton, Marietta Millner, Lia Tora, Yola d'Avril, Mona Rico, Andreé Lafayette, and Lars Hanson were just a handful of the foreigners who couldn't make the transition and whose names are insignificant, almost forgotten today. Bigger stars like Vilma Banky and Emil Jannings were virtually failures in America after sound took over, forcing Banky out of films and Jannings onto a boat back to Germany.

Sam Goldwyn's wife Frances remembered the demise of Banky's career: "Poor dear, she made a number of silent pictures, but that Hungarian accent killed her when sound came in." *Motion Picture Magazine* sadly recalled Banky in March 1932: "Even Vilma Banky doesn't know why she was demoted. They say it was because of her accent."

An ardent fan of Jannings said in a *Photoplay* letter, "I am sorry to hear that Emil Jannings has gone back to Germany, possibly never to return. The talkies are directly responsible for losing the best actor filmland ever had." Jannings would rise again, triumphant, costarring with Marlene Dietrich in Germany's superlative 1930 UFA film, *The Blue Angel.*

Clara Bow, who spoke with a thick Brooklyn accent, had been a huge star. She did not fare well when talkies arrived, in part because her studio (also Paramount) did not prepare her. Her biographer, David Stenn, recalled that a 1931 article in *Photoplay* irked Bow because it assumed she, like Negri, had been "exiled" because of the voice issue. "[Bow] felt her undoing in talkies had not been her voice, but the material."

Anita Page remembered, "It was a time of tragedy and triumph. The tragic part for so many of my contemporaries was that because of their voices not being suited for sound pictures, they were out of a job. Even though some of the stars had achieved great success in silent films and were even idolized by the public, still their careers were over. This was very sad; for some, it meant their whole life was over."

One victim was silent-film leading man John Gilbert. Today his surviving talkies show a competent and well-spoken actor, but the early sound technology and corny dialogue confused and amused the audience, especially the female fans who had idolized him.

Hedda Hopper, who was in Gilbert's first 1929 talkie, *His Glorious Night*, recalled seeing a pathetic John Gilbert onscreen when the film opened in New York. "Jack's first words were 'I love you, I love you, I love you.' With the opening sentence, the audience started to laugh, and he crept out of the theater like a man condemned to the electric chair."

70. John Gilbert and Mae Murray. *The Merry Widow*, 1925.

Silent-film child star Baby Peggy remembered the transition as a "social phenomena" where many former stars could only get work as extras when the studio deemed them unfit for talkies because the early sound technology was so bad. "Many of them committed suicide. Every weekend somebody would walk into the ocean or put their head in a gas oven or run the car in a closed garage until they were overcome with carbon monoxide gas," she recalled.

Julien Fox summed up the transitional period of 1929–30 clearly: "Mexicans—yes; Swedes—yes; Germans—occasionally; French—providing they happened to be Maurice Chevalier or the totally unaccented Claudette Colbert, yes. But Slavs? Very definitely, no."

Latins like Dolores Del Rio and Lupe Velez, Scandinavians like Garbo (and to a lesser extent Nils Asther), and Germans like Dietrich (but not Jannings, whose accent was incomprehensible to many Americans) became or remained popular in the thirties, while Slavs like Banky and Negri were definitely out.

As Emily Wortis Leider wrote, Negri's Polish accent "scared away American directors." Raoul Walsh, who first met Negri when he was assigned to direct her in the 1925 film *East of Suez*, recalled, "I doubt that the man who deciphered the Rosetta Stone could have phoneticized Pola's special brand of English."

But Pola Negri's first talkie performance would happen at last.

A newspaper article on May 10, 1931, announced her imminent return to Hollywood—in a talking picture. She stated that the RKO Pathé Company was prepared to offer her a contract pending her return from Europe. Obviously sensing an uncertain future, she was somewhat philosophical about her return. "When I left these shores two years ago I did not know what was ahead of me, any more than I know now what is before me these coming years in Hollywood."

Another news report appeared May 10, 1931, regarding Negri's move to sound films. Emphasizing the importance of her first talkie, columnist Philip K. Scheuer spoke of the pending RKO contract, which had been offered despite the fact Negri had not yet been heard in a sound movie. "If she had been here when sound first yawped from the screen, it is possible that she would have been summarily released, without even a test, because of her accent. Today, you must understand, accents are fashionable. Garbo, Dietrich, Chevalier made them so."

An article titled "Welcome Back, Pola" observed: "[When] talkies arrived on the scene … she had the good sense to realize immediately that she was through—unless she learned to speak English. Her contract was not renewed … so she left Hollywood bravely and uncompromisingly, without a backward look." The article stated the vaudeville stages in London and Paris had opened up, miraculously clearing up the "English" problem. Negri's voice, "with perhaps just a fascinating suggestion of an accent, will be heard for the first time on the talking screen."

The July 1931 issue of *Picture Play* showed Negri looking somewhat aloof but wrapped beautifully in a fur stole. The caption read, "High resolve lights the sadness of the new Pola, who is determined to become as great a star in talking pictures as she was in silent ones. *Picture Play* has heard her speak—her voice is lovely. Let's all cheer the return of a queenly exile!" The capacity in which the magazine staff "heard" Negri's voice was not explained.

71. "The sadness of the new Pola." *Picture Play*, July 1931.

Another unsourced magazine article from October 1931 reiterated all of the above, stating in short: "She is the same explosive Pola as before."

With much hoopla, Negri's first talkie, *A Woman Commands*, opened on January 29, 1932, at the Mayfair Theater in New York. The film was a historical drama whose plot was adjusted to the needs of the studio. Negri played Madame Maria Draga, and her co-stars were Roland Young, Basil Rathbone, and H. B. Warner. (The actual Maria Draga, the widow of a Czech engineer, served as Queen of Serbia from 1900 to 1903. She and King Alexander I Obrenovich were executed by a group of military officers in 1903.)

Negri needed a hit. This was not to be.

The reviews, though not unfavorable, were tepid. *New York Times* film critic Mordaunt Hall praised "some excellent settings and impressive uniforms," but found the film "hardly exciting ... but is often amusing." He acknowledged Negri's dark vocals. "Her accent is strongly foreign and her voice is a contralto." She had the opportunity to sing in the film; her performance was generally praised by the critics. She went on to record "Paradise," Nacio Herb Brown's hit song from the film.

Variety was not ecstatic either when its review appeared February 2. "Miss Negri is disclosed with a heavy foreign accent, although that was no detriment in a picture of foreign atmosphere." The review also stated, "Her first talker may do fairly well in its RKO New York stand, due to the heavy advance ballyhoo and the presence of Miss Negri in person at the premiere, accompanied by Mayor Walker himself. But when the introductory turmoil and noise are over and picture and star have to go on their way, it will be a different story. Feature promises but thin grosses."

72. Negri with director Paul L. Stein, between takes of *A Woman Commands.* 1932.

A second encapsulated notice in the same issue was even bleaker: "Weak, confused story of 'Zenda' type. Failure of Pola Negri to rise to occasion spells questionable [box office] averages for Polish star's return vehicle."

Unfortunately, not even the hype generated by the appearance of Mayor Jimmy Walker (a celebrity in his own right) could assure the film's success, though his attendance with the star attracted a large and no doubt curious crowd. *A Woman Commands* cost RKO $415,000 to make, what with hiring 2,000 to 5,000 extras and Negri's salary of $30,000 (a huge drop from her glory days at Paramount, where she reportedly received $80,000 per film). The picture was said to have lost $265,000. Although RKO had contracted with Negri for several additional films, this financial fiasco ended that association.

73. A somber portrait of Pola Negri.

Negri's success performing in sound received conflicting reports in *Variety*, whose purpose was to report film grosses and popularity. Seattle, according to *Variety* on February 2, 1932, was using the line "Negri Talks" to publicize *A Woman Commands*, much as MGM did for Garbo's first talkie. *Variety* reported from Minnesota, "Pola Negri out of box office running here. House will do well to top $8,000, bad." The report from San Francisco: "Pola Negri to deplorable $7,000."

As late as April 1932, articles and letters appeared in the fan magazines discussing the quality of the Negri voice. April's *Photoplay* called it "an agreeable, throaty and strongly accented voice." April's *Picture Play*, speaking of her singing, commented that she "warbles in that famous bass-baritone." A fan from Texas wrote in the June *Picture Play*,

"It's the kind of voice you'd expect her to have—deep and husky and full of emotion," and again in June, "the star's voice … it is almost basso."

Interestingly, Negri's autobiography claimed that she had to have an emergency appendectomy after the film's completion and before its release. In her typical dramatic style, she claimed that she was so close to death "a priest came to administer Extreme Unction in a warming, soft chant." A month went by, during which time she was convalescing in Palm Springs. The future was dim, her health so bad that "there was no question of my returning to work for a very long time."

Or was this simply the reason given for a doomed picture and a contract with no further work?

She decided to try performing in vaudeville. *Variety* announced on January 26, just before the release of *A Woman Commands*, that Negri's vaudeville show would start on February 6, 1932, at the Oriental in Chicago. It would simultaneously feature Negri on the big screen *and* live on stage.

74. Negri and nurse after hospitalization.

Perhaps somewhat surprisingly, Negri's initial reviews were very good. *Variety* reported February 9 that while the vaudeville show as a whole ran sloppily (citing a weak comedy act and long dance arrangements), "Miss Negri made good from the bell."

Her act may sound a bit too campy today; but it was a hit with the audience. Negri simply appeared; there was no announcement as the curtains parted. She made "a nifty entrance down center, descending an impressionistic flight of stairs." She then proceeded to give a solo talk on love, also singing, when a man entered the scene. After a "love-wrangle," the two parted ways. Despite the brevity of the story, it "gets all the angles of solid drama, and played without a misstep by the film lady."

Variety's only real complaint was that Negri's low voice had trouble reaching the entire 3,200-seat theater, but this would be remedied once she was "tipped off to pitch her pipes a bit higher." Another notice mentioned that Negri was drawing "a fine femme play," citing her audience as the more matronly type who remembered her when she was "the hottest in celluloid." Further, her own nationality was spurring her on; in the opening days, the Chicago theater was "pulling many of the 450,000 Poles in this town."

Also reported was the fact that Negri's ex-rival for the attentions of Charlie Chaplin, his former wife Lita Grey Chaplin, who was appearing in Syracuse, New York as "The Charming Chantress," had been a no-show for a pre-arranged press preview. This had so alienated the papers that one of her public relations men had to issue "profuse apologies" in order to smooth matters over. No mention was made of whether either of the stars planned to catch the other's performance.

The life of a vaudevillian meant adjusting to different cities, different theaters, and a variety of changes in programs. Negri performed in March at the Paramount Theatre in New York City. This time, the reviewer wasn't as generous in his praise, noting Negri's facial expressions from the distant seats "were hardly discernible." The reviewer found her lines drab and any emotional power lost because "her face was not seen and her voice not heard."

In April she took her act to the Palace Theatre in New York City. There she was praised, in part because her lines were more suitable in that venue than in the larger Paramount.

The show's emcee was a young Milton Berle. According to March 12, 1932, *Variety*, "the nervy kid sold himself all over again with this supposedly sophisticated audience." The trade paper also had a ranking system for "women of the stage" based on a total score of 100. Negri's combined score added up to 83. The article noted that Negri could be improved by "a softer coiffure and more flattering gown."

Negri recalled performing with "a modest but extremely ambitious young comic named Milton Berle" during the week of April 9, 1932. Berle went into detail in his autobiography about having a fling with a "silent-screen vamp" during his vaudeville run. The reference to Negri was evident even though the vamp was unnamed, no doubt to preserve Negri's anonymity since she was still alive. The two shared the same bill; beyond that, how much truth is contained in the comedian's anecdotes is anyone's guess.

75. Negri's Vaudeville program for New York's Palace Theatre. April 9, 1932.

According to Berle, the star spoke and sang "in an accent I've never heard the likes of since." He described her admiration, as she supposedly seduced him in her dressing room, touching his genitals: "Vairy beeg, I tink. And I tink dat is vairy, vairy nice ting to be."

Berle told *Remember* magazine that Negri actually "had an accent you *couldn't* cut with a knife." He said that Negri "was gorgeous and looked terrific onscreen, until the studio realized nobody understood a word of what she was saying."

It was after her first failed American talkie that Berle met her in vaudeville, where supposedly "we got to be very friendly, much friendly, real friendly." The comedian quipped that she returned to Germany to make films under Hitler's regime and "became Hitler's girlfriend. He must have liked her accent. She's the only girl I ever lost to anybody with a mustache."

76. Milton Berle; a vaudevillian romance?

Negri continued to perform and make personal appearances in various cities. *Variety* noted on May 31, 1932, that she had finished her season in vaudeville and would sail for a European vacation. October found her in Minneapolis, where, as it was noted in *Variety*, she "doesn't mean so much to local fans anymore." At the Orpheum, she received a somewhat mixed review, which found her pulling power "problematic." Singing "Paradise" from her film *A Woman Commands,* "she spread the dramatics and vamp business on extra thick."

The consensus found her act unsuited for large vaudeville houses but acknowledged a large amount of applause at her entrance and completion.

As 1932 stretched into 1933, Negri still had no film work. As Negri later recalled, "My stage experience had certainly proved that I was fully capable of speaking dialogue, but what would the reputedly distorting sound recording do to my vocal quality?"

George Schoenbrunn said, "She didn't get any movie offers. What could she do? Sing on the radio? How often could you use a Polish accent in half hour radio shows? There was no money in it."

She found herself doing more personal appearances, including Cincinnati in January 1933, where "her name is all over the theater's exterior and press and poster spreads." *Variety* reported on February 7 that she "disappointed with a sorry $10,500 at the Albee Theatre."

When considering Negri's unimpressive box office results, one has to take into account the economic conditions in America at the height of the Depression. Theatrical shows, concerts, and movies were low on most people's priorities. Nevertheless, the low turnout of paying customers had to be a letdown.

Negri decided to return to Europe. She was prevented from leaving the United States in late February 1933, due to her owing income taxes of "around $80,000 from past earnings in America." The star and the government must have reached a satisfactory resolution, as she was allowed to sail to London on April 7.

77. Negri with her godchild, German actress Johanna von Koczian. Berlin, Wannsee. 1936.

78. Negri and Johanna's mother, Lydia Alexandra von Koczian-Miskolczy.

Negri made one film in France, *Fanatisme*, in 1934, with director Gaston Ravel. She would go on to great success as a talking actress in the mid- to late-thirties in Germany, where her speech was not a concern. She made seven films up through 1938.

David Stewart Hull, author of *Film in the Third Reich*, recalls Negri's arrival in Hitler's Nazi Germany. Hitler's propaganda minister, Joseph Goebbels, accused her of having Jewish heritage. A livid Negri appealed directly to Hitler, who overruled Goebbels, declaring she was "Aryan."

Negri was reportedly one of Hitler's favorite actresses. She recounts in her autobiography how her performance in *Mazurka*, a story about mother love, "would reduce this paradoxically sentimental monster to loud, slobbering tears."

Goebbels's diary entry for November 13, 1935, following the film's premiere: "*Mazurka* by [Willi] Forst with Pola Negri. Really virtuously made. And Negri acts breathtakingly." Perhaps Goebbels had forgiven Negri and reconsidered his accusations.

Mazurka was Negri's first film under the new Nazi regime and her first German-made film since her silent days. It was met with critical acclaim, even causing *Variety* to review the film and ponder on January 1, 1936, what had gone wrong in America. "Pola's comeback into the Teuton film arena is a victorious re-entry. No one has been able to fill that niche which stood vacant ever since her departure for Hollywood some years ago. After this, the unsatisfactory cooperation [between] Negri [and] Hollywood remains more of a mystery than ever."

79. Negri penning her memoirs. May 1934.

How enticing it is to think that, if she had not burnt so many bridges in Hollywood and if she had mastered the English language better, she could have been making glorious cinema for American audiences, especially if she had worked with Ernst Lubitsch as her director!

Perhaps it's best simply to celebrate her magnificent silent-film days, when, for a brief but shining period, Pola Negri was one of the most talented and talked-about stars of her day.

MOTION PICTURE

AUGUST — 25 CTS

A BREWSTER PUBLICATION

Do You Believe
in
Fortune Telling?
See Page 37

Hollywood's
Greatest
Love Story
See Page 2

The Thing That Makes Them Great

80. Negri on the cover of *Motion Picture Magazine*, August 1926.

# SEVEN
COMEBACK, COMEDY, AND CLOSURE

The most amazing thing to me was my reception to my debut in comedy and, more importantly, to my first American film in so many years. To many, I was simply a name remembered by their parents. To others, I was a myth or legend.

—Pola Negri, *Memoirs of a Star*

NEGRI'S MEMOIRS ARE SOMEWHAT vague about the time between her last German-made film and her 1941 return to America. She managed to survive the atrocities of World War II. She spent time in Europe, leaving Berlin and heading for France when the Nazi madness escalated. After traveling through Spain and Portugal, she was finally able to book passage on the *Excalibur* for what she called "an unforgettable crossing" to America.

Though initially barred from re-entering the United States because her visa had lapsed, Negri was finally allowed entry. As far back as the early '20s, Negri had claimed she was going to apply for American citizenship, but had not yet followed through on that intention.

Upon her return to Hollywood, she was considered for the role of Pilar in Ernest Hemingway's *For Whom the Bell Tolls*, but, as with many other opportunities, this fell through and Negri was not cast. Then she had more trouble with the government, which claimed she owed back taxes. Negri explained, "I had earned literally millions and had almost nothing to show for it."

Negri was in desperate need of income. Luckily for her, Andrew Stone was preparing a delightful comedy called *Hi Diddle Diddle* and wanted Negri to play the eccentric opera diva. According to Stone, Negri's agent convinced him to hire her for the colorful role.

Stone recalled in an interview with the author that Negri "was wonderful to work with." They became close friends. He remembered taking her back to Valentino's former estate, Falcon's Lair, where she stayed for some time, thanks to the real estate agent's generosity.

She signed the film contract on April 15, 1943. It stipulated she would receive $2,250.00 "payable to me in cash during production in advance of each week for which the services are to be rendered."

Hi Diddle Diddle was Negri's first real foray into comedy, and she apparently enjoyed the change of pace. "The atmosphere on the set was akin to a children's party, with jokes and laughter and a complete absence of petty jealousies and scene-stealing," she recalled in her memoirs. This was obviously very different from her silent-film days at Paramount.

81. Director Andrew Stone.

Actress June Havoc played a leading role in the film. Though Havoc seldom shared memories of friends, she wrote, "Andy Stone is special." She agreed to answer some questions about the production and, specifically, about working with Negri:

> She hadn't made a film in a long, long time—she was nervous. First day on the set, tacitly, everyone understood, and when she had difficulty remembering her words, Andy didn't say "Cut." He said "Oops, technical problem, sorry—just a minute."

Everyone understood, and in a moment we tried again. But she was still nervous enough to forget her words, so Dennis O'Keefe blurted, "Oh, oh, forgot my lines—sorry, can we please try it again?"

On the third take, Miss Negri was composed and I shall always remember that as a lesson in professionalism of the best sort. Otherwise, she was dignified, glamourous, and cooperative.

In general, the film was quite well received, and Negri received good notices. *Time* seemed very impressed with her comeback when it reviewed the film July 26, 1943. "But [the] highlight of *Hi Diddle Diddle* is the return of … Pola Negri, fabulous vamp of the Rudolph Valentino era." The magazine praised her comedic skills and noted one scene in particular. When Negri, playing opera diva Genya Smetana opposite actor Adolphe Menjou, is urged "not to become violent over Menjou's alleged infidelities, she cries: 'Violent! I'll show you how to be violent'—and launches into an aria from *Tannhaüser*."

82. Adolphe Menjou, Negri in costume for *Hi Diddle Diddle*, 1943.

Not everyone was enamored with the movie, though most critics agreed that the return of Negri was noteworthy. *The New York Times* said the film "reintroduces Pola Negri, the silent-screen queen of vamps, and proves time has neither dimmed her beauty nor improved her acting."

Negri said she received praise for the vocals but acknowledged it was not her own singing. Although her operatic voice was dubbed for the film, that didn't detract from the larger-than-life screwball comedy.

According to Negri's memoirs, her earnings from *Hi Diddle Diddle* allowed her to pay the final installment on her tax assessment. "Whatever the future held, at least I could face it free of debt."

She then left Hollywood and returned to New York. There, around 1944, she first met the woman who would be her companion and friend the rest of her life, Margaret West.

The West family, according to Negri's description, was "enormously wealthy" and owned a lot of property in Texas. Negri and West would spend the remainder of their lives in San Antonio, but initially, according to George Schoenbrunn, Negri and West spent considerable time in Norma Shearer's former Santa Monica home.

83. Negri at Norma Shearer's beach house. 1947.

Schoenbrunn, who first met West in 1947, had very pointed opinions about both ladies and their relationship, sometimes making hostile, accusatory statements. He conceded that West took very good care of Negri, and the two were often spotted at various civic functions and social events around San Antonio.

The women did inspire gossip, as people speculated as to the nature of their relationship. Negri, understandably defensive in discussing her personal life, specifically denied anything sexual in their friendship, despite the remembrances of others that Negri was bisexual.

When Alfred Allan Lewis worked with her on her 1970 autobiography and the subject of West came up, Negri simply told him, "People are so cruel. Always saying Rudy and I are friends—and Margaret and I are lovers—is other way around."

Lewis recalled, "Valentino was, at the least, bisexual—as were both of his wives and probably Pola. The book [Negri's autobiography] tells the Valentino and West episodes the way *Pola* wanted them told, and it was her story from her point of view. And as far as I know—it may have been true… I would like her private life preserved as she imagined it actually was." Where Negri skirted the truth or left out important parts of her life, "I simply invented incidents and characters that covered for her. She was very cooperative and never complained. Whatever suggestions she had for changes in my fiction, I incorporated."

The sexual nature of Negri and West's relationship is irrelevant, in any case. What is important to remember is that West came along when Negri was down on her luck and, as Lewis tactfully put it, offered Negri "love and financial security."

Lewis admired Negri greatly, stating she had always been "kind, generous and thoughtful with me… There was really nothing I didn't like about her. We kept in desultory touch after the book, until she became a recluse."

He particularly liked her dry sense of humor and remembered her excellent martinis. "Every day during our interview sessions, she would stop and, without looking at a watch, say, 'Is noon. Is time for martini.'"

George Schoenbrunn maintained that Negri could be quite nasty after "all her martinis." He presented her as quite a mean-spirited woman to all around her, stating he could well imagine "what a horror she must have been at the studio in her heyday."

In 1951 Negri finally became an American citizen, with help and urging from Schoenbrunn. Both the *Los Angeles Times* and *Los Angeles Examiner* carried her photo with her citizenship papers on January 13, 1951. Schoenbrunn, who had first met Negri in 1943, expressed frustration she had not become an American citizen sooner, as "she always wrapped herself up in the American flag."

He recalled that he got a teacher for her, and Negri "made a fuss having to learn the little bit of American history … I told her, 'You are an actress [and] can surely remember the amendments and the presidents. Think what I had to learn in Europe history!' … She passed the exam, of course, and Margaret and I were witnesses—me not being mentioned in her book, which was so typical for her."

Others familiar with Negri and West in San Antonio also recalled the star. In her late years, Negri "always played hard to get." Her appearances around San Antonio became fewer and fewer, but she was definitely noticed when she did appear in public.

Tom Cook first met them in 1957. Employed as an usher for the San Antonio Symphony Society, he greeted the two women and ensured their privacy. He had to wait until all the audience members had left, and then he was allowed to "escort them out to meet their driver on the front steps." He recalled:

> They were very generous patronesses of the orchestra and annual spring Grand Opera Festival produced by the San Antonio Symphony. In public, Pola was always "the great star"—a tiny waif, almost bird-like creature. Always gowned in bias-cut black slipper satin, 1930s style. Her jet-black hair cut in a severe "shingle-bob" and enough diamonds to open a branch office of Harry Winston.
>
> [At] after-performance parties, the persona remained the same. I don't think Pola Negri knew the meaning of the word "relax." She was always "on."
>
> One of my jobs as head usher was to greet her—always "Good evening, Madame—NEVER address her by name in the theater. And to be damn sure that the media never got within spitting distance of her box.
>
> Pola was very generous in her support financially but also very closeted socially. She never entertained in her suite at the Menger Hotel and rarely gave parties at the Argyle Club. She was a much sought-after guest—but rarely a hostess.
>
> Pola Negri was very kind to me—to Margaret West I was invisible, a non-entity. Every Christmas, Pola would give me an envelope—inside was a one hundred dollar bill—no card, no note, just the money. This was like manna from heaven to a teenaged student.
>
> I really don't think any of them ever knew my name.

Concerning Valentino, she was always absent from San Antonio around the anniversary of Rudolph's death. And when she came out in public, she always carried a single, *perfect* red rose.

Margaret King Stanley was president of San Antonio's Symphony League in the early '70s when she first met Negri. "I have nice memories of her, and Pola was honored at our gala."

84. Negri, Mayor Walter McAllister, Margaret King Stanley. San Antonio Symphony League, 1972.

Another acquaintance, Jo An Rogers, was present at a wedding Negri had been invited to. "I don't remember her talking to anyone, and she wouldn't sign the bride's book!" Negri always guarded her private life in San Antonio, and when Rogers saw her at the hairdresser's, "there were curtains all around her so she couldn't be seen!"

As for Schoenbrunn, his relationship with Negri was at times strained. He expressed frustration with all of her personal drama and was, perhaps rightfully, upset at not being mentioned in her book. She was, however, generous to him, often sending him monetary gifts.

"She always sent me checks of one hundred or two hundred dollars for Christmas and my birthdays," he recalled. "I had numerous meals with her at Margot's"—Margaret's—"villa, stayed with them at the Racquet Club in Palm Springs, the Sands in Las Vegas, and the Biltmore in Santa Monica, but had to pay dearly, being public and [personal] psychiatrist and legal and spiritual counselor, rolled in one."

85. Margaret West and Negri. 1950's, Palm Springs.

Schoenbrunn was kind enough to locate several of Negri's early films and materials abroad, including a copy of her German-made film *Mazurka*. "I also found an old score of 'Paradise' which cost a lot, which I gave her and received barely a thank you ... I was never invited to San Antonio, typical of Pola. She said it would be too compromising were I to stay in her townhouse. I said I could put up at the Menger Hotel, but no. I'm glad I never went there."

On July 29, 1963, Margaret West died. According to Negri's memoir, she was understandably devastated by the loss of her good friend and provider.

As Negri's ghostwriter, Lewis, recalled, "Pola was a very nice, kind, and sad lady ... West was dead, [Negri] was lonely and forgotten by the time I worked with her. This—I think you'll agree—is sufficient grounds for sadness."

West's Last Will and Testament, dated June 6, 1961, left West's estate in Olmos Park, San Antonio, to Negri "so long as she lives and desires to occupy said home." West bequeathed to Negri all the contents of the home, plus a diamond cross, a diamond ring, and "all of my pearls." Negri also received trust income of $1250 per month for life.

The generosity of West left Negri financially secure and comfortable for the remainder of her life, which was spent in the home they had shared in San Antonio.

Around this time Negri was offered the role of Madame Habib in Walt Disney's *The Moon-Spinners,* which would be her great and final comeback. Negri's memoirs imply that she accepted the Disney role largely due to Margaret's wishes.

Schoenbrunn's description of events is telling and amusing:

> An English writer friend, Michael Dyne, adapted *The Moon-Spinners* for Disney, and I told him to get Pola a part in it. He spoke to Disney, who said, "But she's been dead for years." I gave them all the colored, recent photos I had of her, and she got the part.
>
> She wanted fifty thousand, but only got half. She wanted me to accompany her to London and get me a part in the movie. I knew what that would entail and didn't go with her. I met her then in London before shooting began. She said she would never stay at the Dorchester, so I called the Savoy, Connaught, Ritz, Claridge's. Of course, she was at the Dorchester. I finally got through to her, as she was getting so grand again. [I] had dinner with her, and I will say that though both Dietrich and Bardot were also staying there at the same time, she got all the publicity.

Schoenbrunn recalled that Pola Negri got a lot of publicity compared to the young Hayley Mills, who played a major character in the film. Schoenbrunn was not exaggerating. The announcement of Negri's Disney comeback made news in every major newspaper and magazine.

Hollywood's gossip queen and actress Hedda Hopper broke the news in the *Los Angeles Times* on August 15, 1963. Expressing surprise, she reported, "Our greatest siren … is making her return in, of all things, a Walt Disney picture. Pola is going to outdo Liz's Cleo by sailing into the Bay of Dolphins on Crete on a luxurious yacht to make contact with that old jewel thief Wallach."

The *Los Angeles Times* reported out of San Antonio on August 18 that "the flame of Rudolph Valentino and a star of the silent screen is coming out of retirement after eighteen years." Negri, it added, had been spending the intervening time writing her autobiography and traveling. "I have a great story to tell in my autobiography," she was quoted. Praising her slim figure, black hair, and green eyes, the article stated the announcement came "only a few days after she was willed the plush home of Mrs. Margaret West in Olmos Park, a suburb of San Antonio."

In addition, *United Press International* Hollywood correspondent Vernon Scott reported on August 22 that Negri, "the Elizabeth Taylor of her time," would be making her comeback at age sixty-three. "Hollywood's changed so much I hardly recognize it," Negri stated in her "heavy European accent." But she was glad to be back, as she missed her acting career. Scott recalled her glory days, when she was the first to paint her toenails with red polish. These days, however, Negri stated that she lived alone and was kept busy with civic work and writing. "I go to see a good many movies and find that today's actresses aren't as exciting as we once were."

Articles continued to appear almost monthly in the *New York Times, Los Angeles Times, Variety, Film Daily, Los Angeles Herald Examiner*, and magazines as well. In May 1964, Negri was interviewed in the *Los Angeles Times* by Philip K. Scheuer and seemed to express no regret with her career. "Your vogue passes. I never live in the past." She talked about the telegram that arrived offering her the part in the Disney film and how movies were her "original love." She mentioned Valentino and how he could have lived "if they had had penicillin in those days."

When Louella Parsons interviewed Negri in May 1964 for the *Herald Examiner*, Negri expressed surprise that she was being remembered and honored. "So many people thought I was dead—it's just wonderful, all these magnums of champagne arriving at my hotel suite." Reminiscing about the early days of Hollywood, Negri quipped, "We were treated like kings and queens—but when we worked we worked like dogs. Twelve hours a day, six days a week. We didn't have Equity or the Screen Actors Guild to protect us. But we had great times."

Negri's reception upon arriving in London to begin production on *The Moon-Spinners* was covered intensely by the press. Her memoirs recount some fascinating headlines and articles. *The London Daily Mirror* headlined its report: "The Greatest Vamp of Them All Flew Into London Last Night." But perhaps the riveting description in the *London Evening News* by William Hall best sums up the excitement and glamour of a time long departed. "To the adulators, the adorers, the admirers thronging the Gold Room, Miss Negri brought the dear, dead, golden days of Hollywood back for one sweet moment."

Film historian Kevin Brownlow was present when Negri arrived in London for filming. He waited for her entrance at the press reception in the Gold Room of the Dorchester Hotel, and he gave this vivid account of the crowd's excitement and curiosity.

It was crammed with pressmen, gossip columnists and publicity people. The young ones were clustered eagerly around the veterans, hearing about the fabulous figure who was soon to arrive. Her photographs lined the walls, publicity handouts referred to her romances with Chaplin and Valentino and recalled her triumphs in post-World War I Germany.

Suddenly, there was a commotion in the corridor outside. The Gold Room was emptied of everyone but me. I hardly dared to go outside, afraid she must have changed so much. I waited a few seconds longer than anyone else, then I shot outside. And craning over the heads of cameramen, I caught my first glimpse of Pola Negri. She was standing in an aristocratic pose, holding a leash, at the end of which strained a cheetah. A real, live cheetah.

86. Negri and cheetah at press conference for *The Moon-Spinners.*

The scene was authentic 1920s Hollywood. She was 66, but she looked 46. And even if the idea of bringing over the cheetah was inspired by the fact it would appear with her in *The Moon-Spinners*, it seemed the sort of splendid damn fool stunt she'd have done at a '20s premiere.

And, of course, the press went mad. Every time the cheetah yawned (it was too soporific to growl) the cameraman leaped back several yards.

Miss Negri was in command and let it be known that this was not a comeback. "I hate that word," she said. "This is my return to pictures after many very successful years in Texas real estate."

She turned down all television interviews, saying, "TV I hate."

I knew Andrew L. Stone, the director who had worked with Negri, so I asked him to intervene on my behalf. Unfortunately, he forgot to call her. He made up for it twelve years later.

Actor Eli Wallach had much to say about Negri's comeback in a handwritten reply to the author. He had never met Negri prior to *The Moon-Spinners*, but he recalled seeing her screen performances. "Mostly her eyes were rimmed with black and she was always lying on a divan, like Manet's painting."

He worked with Negri "only two or three days" on *The Moon-Spinners*, not long enough to know her well. But Wallach found her presence very interesting and exciting.

Most of the film was shot on the island of Crete; after three months there, we went to Pinewood [Studio] outside London and worked for about two weeks.

We were merely told she'd be part of the Pinewood shooting. Curiosity was the biggest reaction. She was alive! And happy to be back before the cameras. I still don't know how they found her and convinced her to come back.

She looked great. She'd arrive very early at Pinewood in a long Rolls, all curtains drawn, and leap out of the car and into makeup. An hour and a half later she'd appear—lovely to look at. NO ONE saw her, except the chauffeur, before filming.

Very vivid in my mind was the scene on Ms. Negri's yacht where she was buying the "jooolls"—that's how she pronounced it. The fact she was alive—

alert and keenly interested in movies and theater. And that she was living in retirement in Texas. Cagney made a comeback after a long retirement in *Ragtime* and there was a lot of publicity about that. But Pola topped all retirements. She had been out of the limelight for years. And now here she was—Valentino's silent mourner, back before the public. Like *Sunset Boulevard*—she was still big—the movies had gotten smaller!

She probably never knew who the hell I was. After all, I was basically a New York stage actor. She did not discuss her early career. I guess she figured we knew all about her. Neither me nor Ms. Negri were intimidated. After all, she was a pro. She was certainly a survivor and a pleasure to act with. Whenever people interview me about films I've been in, I take great pleasure in trying to make them guess what famous legend I worked with. My answer is always met with disbelief. "Pola Negri," I shout. "Pola Negri!"

87. Negri around the time of *The Moon-Spinners*. 1964.

George Shoenbrunn's reminiscences continued with Negri's return from the London filming session.

> She sent me as a present a golden fountain pen from Asprey's, an elegant shop on Bond Street. When she returned she called me to say that she was to get an Oscar for the film. It was in November, while the nominations occur in January!

> She came here, lunched at Disney's and came back screaming in German, Polish, and English that they cut her part to nothing and what a lousy director Anderson was, etc. [Actually, the director was James Neilson; Bill Anderson was the co-producer.]

> A couple of weeks later she phones from San Antonio, to say that [Gregory] Peck had called her to come here for the Oscars. I should hire a limousine, book a suite at the Beverly Wilshire, etc. I knew the director of the Oscars, who told me that there was not the slightest chance of her getting an Oscar. That year they had invited all the still-living silent stars, and the camera would only focus on her for a few seconds. I called her back and warned her, and so she refused the invitation, which didn't make her any more popular in Hollywood.

> She was nothing in the film, did not even look good and was badly dressed.

The Moon-Spinners opened on July 8, 1964. When Negri's autobiography came out six years later, in 1970, it naturally created a lot of press.

The Hollywood Reporter's Radie Harris plugged Negri's memoir on June 12, 1970. "Alfred Allan Lewis, a brilliant writer, worked directly with Miss Negri for two years in preparation of these four hundred forty-six fascinating pages."

However, Harris remarked on Negri's lack of promotion for the book. When she was in public, "she was so heavily veiled you could hardly see her." And after leaving New York to return to San Antonio, "she has done nothing to promote her book via TV shows or other interviews."

When Harris asked why Negri would not publicize the book more, Lewis replied, "First of all she is self-conscious about her accent, which after all these years remains as heavy as ever."

Lewis recalled her hesitancy at promoting her book and doing interviews when it was released. "Pola feared her accent and bad grammar would make people think she hadn't written the book. She preferred to do the Garbo bit and not be available. She lost both of us a great deal of money ... On publication day, she was interviewed by Angela Taylor for the *New York Times*. After speaking to her, Taylor could not believe she wrote the book and demanded to know [if] I'd written it. I did not reply."

88. Negri at a New York book signing for her autobiography.

Acclaimed book editor Larry (Lawrence) Ashmead, who was responsible for Negri's book and signed Lewis to cowrite it, recalled Lewis having to fill in gaps where Negri's story was incomplete. "Alfred invented a girlfriend so we could put in some conversation. Pola was very vague about her childhood and I got the impression the family was rather poor."

Still, Ashmead said, "I really did like her! She was always the star!" He was delighted when the *New York Daily News* printed a photo of Negri and Ashmead, even though "I wasn't identified."

Lewis recalled that as far as Negri's childhood, "I was completely dependent upon Pola. I did embellish to fill out characters, scenes, and settings."

"Her book," countered Schoenbrunn, "is nothing but a bunch of lies and no interesting stories about co-actors, directors, or lovers in detail."

Lewis pointed out: "Adela Rogers St. Johns went on the *Tonight Show* and voluntarily called it the best book ever to come out of Hollywood. The book was a great success in France and Poland."

The *Los Angeles Times* calendar section of August 9, 1987, recalled the occasion when the Academy of Motion Picture Arts and Sciences had honored Valentino on the fiftieth anniversary of his death. Fay Kanin, acclaimed screenwriter and later president of the Academy, had read a telegram from Negri that astounded the audience. Negri wrote, "We miss beloved Rudy. He was a true star. I applaud your homage. Signed, Pola Negri."

A gasp erupted from those present, not so much in reaction to the content of her message, "but that Pola Negri was still alive." Yes, she was very much alive in 1976 and remembering her beloved Rudolpho.

89. Negri in 1948. New York. Valentino's portrait displayed.

Negri became somewhat of a recluse in her later years. But she definitely was not for-gotten after she left films for good and made a comfortable life in San Antonio. Negri was always good for a story, continually showing up in the press whether film-related or not, almost right up to her death in 1987.

"She got fan mail every single day. We'd always open up packages," said Loretta Ellerbee, Negri's caregiver during the 1980s.

90. Negri with Patrick Mahony (facing) and George Schoenbrunn. Santa Barbara, late 1950's.

Ellerbee remembers Negri telling her stories about how her maid would pack her lunch basket during the '20s. And all of Negri's luggage—"red leather, and lots of it."

When Pope John Paul II became the first non-Italian pope in 1978, Negri was "thrilled because he was a Pole."

Two of Negri's favorite restaurants in San Antonio were Paesano's, an Italian restau-rant, and Earl Abel's. "The owner of Paesano's would go out to the car to greet her," Ellerbee said.

Ellerbee recalled that Negri liked to be driven around in Loretta's old Cadillac, and added these reminiscences:

I played these eight-tracks in the car of polka music, and Miss Negri's legs would be moving from her knees down! She knew how to dance ... She could dance, she could sing a little, [and] she was quite an actress.

But she was extremely self-conscious about her accent. She thought she spoke like the rest of Americans. It's just her voice didn't transcribe well into talkies.

She'd call my mom, in that heavy accent which was her downfall. She didn't make it because of her accent; she couldn't get rid of it. She'd say she spoke six languages. Polish first, then French, German, English, Russian, and a little Italian.

When I knew her, she was a hard-hitter, gin and tonic, perhaps cocaine in her younger life in the fast lane. The doctor told me it wasn't the gin that would eventually take its toll; it was all that tonic water! Imagine that! She looked forward to five o'clock that's for sure.

She was also a big egg-eater; she liked them soft-boiled, like her old girlfriend Mae Murray, yolk and all.

She liked to exaggerate and make the story worth telling ... She claimed her birth certificate burned up, the whole court house burned up! She [was] a victim of her own imagination and she became reclusive because people don't want to put up with that foolishness anymore. That star treatment and all? They don't want that. That's '30s.

There were so many nurses and maids who came in and out. She called me her "manager" because she didn't want a nurse. I've never been around anyone who was that spoiled.

She did not like to bathe every day; she was very European.

She had such small and delicate feet and hands. Her favorite color was jonquil yellow.

Her condo had three bedrooms and three baths plus a huge kitchen. Also, a small den where we spent most of our time. And she'd sit right up in front of the television and try to see it. But she said the Klieg lights had ruined her eyes.

This was a common thread echoed by silent-film stars. Even director Andrew Stone remembered the bright lights. "I received a serious infection from them. But the studios managed to soften down the glare so in later times they were okay."

Kevin Brownlow explained the so-called Klieg eyes affliction. "It was not an infection. When cameramen needed as much light as they could get, they had the gaffer remove the glass from the arc lights. The glass cut down ultra-violet rays. Without it, the actors suffered from a painful inflammation which could only be relieved by lying in the dark for hours."

Negri's longtime lawyer Gilbert Denman recalled that she talked about her career and that Golden Era all the time, "but spoke only of Pola Negri." In Denman's association with her, Negri remembered Chaplin and Valentino fondly. "She denied the romance with Hitler and spoke kindly of Swanson and claimed she and Swanson were close friends." He concurred that he liked her very much but said he did not want "to get into our professional or personal relationship."

Before her death in 2008, silent star Anita Page corresponded with the author. Although Miss Page would not comment on whether or not she felt Valentino and Negri had been involved in a heated romance, she offered the following insights into Negri and the wonderful years when they had made silent films:

> I had occasions where Pola and I met. I remember she was very much the grand screen actress, even in person, and why not? After all, it was rather expected of most of us. Her reputation, much like her screen image, was one of glamour. She played it to the hilt! I admired that, also I found her to be nice, I liked that too!

> My close friend and ex-husband, Nacio Herb Brown, knew her and worked with her on some music for one of her pictures. He arranged for Pola and I to meet and have lunch a couple of times. She was fascinating! She loved being a movie star, so did I! I would say that the 1920s Hollywood, as well as the '30s Hollywood, was an exciting time of celebrities and many social functions that a film star was expected to attend.

> Of course, the loss of Rudy Valentino was one of the great tragedies of that era. Partly because he was so young, that's always sad, but also because of what he meant to so many. He, like so many of our early movie idols, could not be replaced. He was an original in a period of history when we were all

creating something for the first time. Now they call it the Golden Era. How marvelous for me to have been a part of that!"

On May 27, 1977, Kevin Brownlow had his opportunity to see Negri again, at a screening of her film *A Woman of the World*, hosted by Patrick Monaghan. Also present were researcher Sue McConachy, director Curtis Harrington, and David Bradley, who had agreed to show the film.

What follows is how Brownlow described the night and his quest to obtain Negri's consent to record an interview with him. (The author has added attribution where needed for clarity.)

> She was dressed in pure white—a white fur wrap, white pearls and over-made-up lips a la 1940. She looked grotesque after too many face lifts. She still had a heavy Polish accent. She was helped up the stairs and it was hastily explained that she was near-sighted. She was introduced, and behind her was Andrew L. Stone, with his new wife.
>
> I soon found myself sitting to the right of Negri, uncomfortable at first and trying my best to initiate conversation about her legendary career. I asked her how long it had been since she'd seen *A Woman of the World*.
>
> "Four years. At Museum of Modern Art, for my book," she replied.
>
> "It is a very funny picture," I offered.
>
> She launched into exactly the same story I had heard at Claridge's in 1966, when she was meeting the press in 1966—how she was on stage from eight, and Max Reinhardt came to Warsaw mysteriously occupied by the Germans *after* the war and cast her in *Sumurun* with Lubitsch as the hunchback. "Yes, you have read it in my book," she said.
>
> Now she was chilly and ordered me to get her wrap.
>
> Mrs. Stone brought up the Minelli film she was asked to do but turned down, *A Matter of Time* (1976). "Ingrid Bergman wasn't right," said Mrs. Stone.
>
> "Dahlink, it was about famous courtesan. Liza Minelli is talented but utterly miscast—it is disaster," Negri replied.

I asked her about *Sunset Boulevard.* "Were you not offered that and did you not turn it down?"

"No—because if I had been offered it I should have grabbed it." Negri suddenly laughed, and a hint of self-deprecation broke through the mask. Others tried to make her agree to appear in another film. "Sometimes I feel I must—I long for it—then next morning, I wake up—absolutely no."

I tried to tell her how interested young people were in silent films, but it went without effect.

"But what is there now? The pornography is simply dreadful. I mean, I think sex is beautiful, but it must be presented properly with taste, don't you agree?" she asked.

Curtis Harrington agreed. Negri asked me if I agreed.

To deflect her, I said, "Just think of what we'll be seeing in twenty years' time. We'll look back and laugh. But perhaps the pendulum will swing back."

Curtis Harrington said fashion would change. "It usually goes in cycles. I am planning a romantic film next. Iris Murdoch's *The Unicorn.*" He brought up the phenomenon of audiences reacting against violence—ironic from a maker of horror films.

I tried to steer the conversation back to the fascination that young people have when they see old films. I realized *old* was the wrong word.

"Silent films." No response.

Ah, it needed to be personalized. I told her I was fascinated by silent films—a flicker. That it was one of her performances that aroused my enthusiasm. Success.

She clutched my arm. "Oh, that's wonderful. Dahlink, tell me, which one of my performances was it?"

"*The Spanish Dancer.*"

"Ah, yes."

"Herbert Brenon directed it. Did you get on well with him, or did he try to act everything out for you?"

A ripple of laughter from Negri. "I did not get on with Herbert Brenon, but it was a good picture, despite everything. Have you seen *Forbidden Paradise?*"

"Only three reels—the rest does not exist," I said.

"Oh, I would give my right arm for a print of that," said Negri.

I told her about the rich potential of the archives in Iron Curtain countries.

"Maybe Poland, yes? My book is in paperback—paperback—and it sold half a million."

"My goodness," said I, surprised because I had heard it had done so poorly. "That's far better than any of the others."

"Yes!" she said, with emphasis.

And then I realized that all I had to do was to pile on the flattery. I hated doing that as a rule, because it sounds so insincere, yet it seemed the only way.

"Do you feel if you had stayed in Europe, you might have made another *Madame DuBarry?*" I knew this was her favorite.

"But I made many big pictures—*Carmen*, for Lubitsch, *Madame DuBarry*, known as *Passion* in America, it was a tremendous success. And in America you forget *Barbed Wire.*"

I could exult with sincerity over that, but she wasn't interested in my memories of Rowland V. Lee. I thought a little more flattery was in order. "You made a great statement against war in that."

"Yes, I did," she said, to my surprise.

I brought up the name of [Erich]Pommer, which elicited a strong response.

"Ah, Pommer, a genius. Yes, he did have a lot to do with *Barbed Wire* and *Hotel Imperial*. He produced them." That was another of her favorites, *Hotel Imperial*.

91. *Barbed Wire*, 1927. Negri, Emil Jannings, director Rowland V. Lee.

I tried to ask her if she regretted coming to America.

She seemed surprised. "I was not only a silent star in America. I was a talking star from 1935 in Germany."

"Er … yes," I said. "Why is it that none of the other German stars who came to America were successful—de Putti, Camilla Horn …?"

"They may have been beautiful," replied Negri. "They were not talented. Sometimes I look at a good film on TV and I am proud to have been part of the industry—an important part."

Then I said, "I would like you to do me a great favour—and appear in front of a motion picture camera once more."

Negri replied, "I do not understand."

I pressed on. "I would like to ask you to appear once more in front of a motion picture camera—for me—to talk about Lubitsch, about *Madame DuBarry*, how you changed history by coming to the USA—you changed the entire history of the motion picture …"

"I could never appear in public again," said Negri. "It would make me physically ill. I am sorry."

I countered, "But you would not be acting. It would be like this, a conversation—with a camera."

But no. "I am sorry, I could not do it. It would make me too emotional. I told you, sometimes I look at films and long to go back, but next morning I wake up and no. You understand?" she asked Curtis Harrington.

Curtis Harrington said, "I understand."

"You're supposed to be a director," I told him. "Stop saying you understand."

I explained what we were doing, tribute to the silents, etc. Still she refused. "You can't say no. I've come all this way from England just to get to you." I suggested sound only, and that took her aback, but then she came up with another lengthy alibi.

"I have turned down many requests for interviews, but never have I confessed the reason, as I confess to you." And she went into a long description of the trouble with her eyes—"retinitis"—and how she could not see four inches in front of her and therefore could not read. (Curiously, she could see the film when David Bradley ran it, and complained that it had been cut since she last saw it.)

"But you wouldn't need to read."

By this time she was two or three inches from my face. The electricity was so strong as she clutched my arm that I said, "But don't you love those films, don't you love those days?"

"I do, I do—but I cannot—you understand."

I mentioned Olga Petrova—"someone who retired before you came into pictures"—and her successful eye operation.

"She is much older than me," said La Negri indignantly, and I nearly lost her.

I tried another tack. "Gloria Swanson is refusing."

"But she is on TV all the time."

"Yes, but she only talks about health foods."

Pola laughed. She clearly relished hearing Swanson, her old rival, put down. As if to confirm the stories of the Swanson-Negri feud, she said, "I hate cats." Disney wanted her to have a cat on a leash at the press conference. "It was my idea to have a cheetah. It is in my book. It was front page news for days."

In order to keep pace with La Negri, I was swallowing glass after glass of champagne. I realized the only way of succeeding in what was, after all, a seduction, was to prostitute myself. I felt shame even as I spoke. "There were only two superstars in those days—you and Garbo."

"That's true," replied Negri, "but there was also Dietrich."

"She came later," I answered.

"Oh, you mean in my era?"

"Yes."

"Garbo was very beautiful …"

I caught the drift and prostituted myself further. "But you were by far the greater actress."

The arm came out and clutched mine. "Thank you, my dear," she said, as if she had been waiting for this. "Garbo was beautiful, but she played the same in every picture. She was not a great actress."

I swallowed more champagne, feeling that lightning should strike me. But I was certainly making a hit with Pola. "How did you get on with Marion Davies?" I asked.

"Ah, Marion was my friend. When Rudy died, the first people to arrive to comfort me were Marion Davies and William Randolph Hearst. If that is not friendship …" She adopted a tragic expression, rather like the one she wore at the funeral.

Long pause.

92. Negri, circa 1982. San Antonio.

"Do you keep in touch with Valentino's brother?" I asked.

"No. Where is he? He used to be a bookkeeper at MGM," Negri said.

She talked of San Antonio and her favourite university, St. Mary's. How she gave them her films, how she liked the fiesta, the dancing, the gardens.

"Where are the cattle ranches?" I asked.

She told me her friends the Wests owned 40,000 acres. She wore western out-fits and rode to corral horses and cattle.

[The screening of] *A Woman of the World* was received with laughter in the funny bits and in some of the not so funny bits. Patrick accompanied it with records, decidedly ill-chosen, such as Fred Astaire songs.

The clock clanged every quarter of an hour. Pola refused to sign books be-cause she hadn't got her glasses (very clever!).

At the end of the evening, Patrick said it had gone exactly as he'd hoped. But I had failed.

I was ill during the night, thanks to the champagne, and next morning could not move. I had to abandon all hope of going to interview Dolores Costello and Neil Hamilton, and I was bitterly disappointed—particularly because this would be my only chance of meeting them.

But at least I had met Pola Negri!

Although Kevin Brownlow felt he had failed, I believe it was Negri who had failed, failed all of us by not granting him an interview. The information she could have supplied would have been priceless. Sadly, that book of intriguing information was closed forever, ten years later.

? see p. 151

Pola Negri passed away on August 1, 1987. She died of complications from pneumonia and an untreated brain tumor. Her obituary was carried in almost every newspaper in America, as well as abroad.

Gail Owen, a San Antonio resident at the time, recalled the rosary service held for Negri in San Antonio, which was attended by around two hundred people. "Her casket was open. She was laid out in a gold silk tunic with a white turban. I especially remember the red lipstick and fingernails. She looked very elegant for her early nineties."

Columnist Paula Allen of the San Antonio Express-News reported Negri was buried in a silver-colored casket. "A rose and a peacock feather (both allusions to her accounts of her affair with Valentino) were placed in with her." Negri also had requested she be buried with "the platinum wedding band I always wear." The ring's provenance was not noted in Negri's will, according to Allen.

Following the rosary service, Negri's body was flown to Los Angeles. There she was entombed in a crypt next to her mother in Calvary Cemetery.

93. Negri's crypt at Calvary Cemetery.

Richard Cox attended the service in California and was surprised by how few people were present. "There were about six or eight other people, one of whom was [actor] Roddy McDowall. I recall thinking at the time it was rather sad so few people were there—on the outskirts of Hollywood—to mourn Pola's passing. It seemed to sum up the life of a fallen and forgotten film icon."

Negri's lawyer, Gilbert Denman, Jr., stated Negri's estate was "very modest," but she made generous provisions to St. Mary's University, the San Antonio Symphony, Trinity University, and several charities and individuals. Her large portrait of Valentino, which he had given her during their courtship, was left to Valentino's nephew, Jean. Her will also stipulated that a trust fund be established for a ten-dollar bouquet of flowers to be placed every Christmas, Easter, and Mother's Day at the crypt she shared with her mother.

Author Marjorie Rosen crystallized the essence of Negri's unique persona: "A legend even in her own time, Pola Negri conjures up all the exoticism that was Hollywood in the '20s. Yet we overlook her talent and forget her considerable positive contributions to this genre simply because most of us immediately assume that Negri, the last of the [Theda] Bara heirs, was cast from the same kohl-and-asp mold."

Eugene V. Brewster's remarks in the July 1926 issue of *Motion Picture Classic* are perhaps the most astute observation of Negri's legacy:

> I believe Pola Negri is one of the most admired of all women of the screen, but I am now inclined to think that she will never be so popular in real life as are many others, because the average man does not usually fall in love with intellectual women, and women don't often take kindly to those of their sex who are smarter than they are.

> While Pola is not a masculine woman, she is the exact opposite of the Lillian Gish type. One would never liken Pola to the fragile lily nor to the delicate violet. She is more than a flower—she is a sturdy oak, full of life, strength and power.

> If one had never seen her on the stage or screen, one would feel safe to bet that she was a great artiste and that she will be just that, long after many others now in her general class are dead and buried.

94. Pola Negri. Portrait by Donald Biddle Keyes.

FILMOGRAPHY

Pola Negri in American Cinema

Bella Donna

95. *Bella Donna.* Negri with Conrad Nagel. 1923.

Released April 1, 1923. Famous Players–Lasky Corporation.

Distribution: Paramount Pictures. 8 reels (7,895–7,903 feet).

Director: George Fitzmaurice.

Producer: Adolph Zukor.

Writers: Ouida Bergère (scene), Robert Smythe Hichens (story).

Cinematography: Arthur C. Miller.

Art Direction/Production: Dudley Stuart Corlett.

Cast

Pola Negri (Bella Donna/Mrs. Ruby Chepstow), Conway Tearle (Mahmoud Baroudi), Conrad Nagel (Nigel Armine), Adolphe Menjou (Mr. Chepstow), Claude King (Dr. Meyer Isaacson), Lois Wilson (Patricia), Macey Harlam (Ibrahim), Robert Schable (Dr. Hartley).

Synopsis

After her husband is convicted of throwing one of her suitors into a Venetian canal, adventuress Bella Donna (Mrs. Ruby Chepstow) marries engineer Nigel Armine, they travel to Egypt, and she becomes smitten by Mahmoud Baroudi, who persuades her to poison Nigel. Once accused, she flees to Baroudi, now with another woman. She returns to Nigel, now being cared for by his former sweetheart. Bella Donna wanders into a desert sandstorm, alone.

"Some things they did on *Bella Donna* were quite appalling. I was ashamed to have my name on it. That's when I decided I would get out of the business."

—Ouida Bergère

Reviews

A simple tale for simple people, but sure to fill the eye and mind of the usual picture house patrons ... Pola Negri seems to have some particular draw over here. Whether it was lately gained through publicity or that the sex-mad public believes Negri is symbolic of the diabolical is just guesswork. They [Famous Players] have improved upon Negri in appearance ... but they didn't improve upon her methods of registration. Her scheme for anguish appears to be a line drawn across her cheek and a drop of glycerine under her left eye. One-eye criers are new over here.
—*Variety*, April 5, 1923

Pola Negri's first American-made picture does not fit her as well as those tailored in Berlin. Pola is more beautiful but less moving; a passion flower fashioned into a poinsettia. The picture is thoroughly artificial.
—*Photoplay*, July 1923

According to *Motion Picture Magazine* of August 1923, *Bella Donna* was a failure, and Charlie Chaplin upset Pola Negri by telling her she was "punk" in it.

Herewith I want to protest against the "Paramountization" of Pola Negri, as shown in *Bella Donna*. She was our favorite screen actress, not because we are not loyal Americans, but because we believe that art is international, and genius an accident of birth anywhere! ...We had read glowing accounts of how Hollywood makeup and superior photography would make Pola even more alluring than ever ... But what did we see? A poor imitation of Gloria Swanson and other standardized heroines of the Lasky mould into which the gorgeous Pola was pressed and her art suppressed! Why, she was even made to drop her easy, erect, natural carriage and to walk like Gloria, with her shoulders hunched up and her head down between them like a panther, giving an outward curve to her chest. Oh, Pola, how could you? The others know not what they do, but you know! Go back to Europe, Pola, and save your art, before it is crushed into the "dumbbell" mould.

—Letter from a fan (M. L. McLean, Los Angeles) in *Photoplay*, October 1923

Hollywood

Released August 19, 1923. Famous Players–Lasky Corporation.
Distribution: Paramount Pictures. 8 reels (8,100 feet).
Director: James Cruze.
Producer: Jesse L. Lasky.
Writers: Tom Geraghty (adaptation), Frank Condon (story).
Cinematography: Karl Brown.

Cast

Hope Drown (Angela Whitaker), Luke Cosgrave (Joel Whitaker), George K. Arthur (Lem Lefferts), Ruby Lafayette (Grandmother Whitaker), Harris Gordon (Dr. Luke Morrison), Bess Flowers (Hortense Towers), Eleanor Lawson (Margaret Whitaker), King Zany (Horace Pringle), Roscoe "Fatty" Arbuckle (Fat man in casting director's office).

Stars and celebrities: Gertrude Astor, Mary Astor, Agnes Ayres, Baby Peggy, T. Roy Barnes, Noah Beery, William Boyd, Clarence Burton, Robert Cain, Edythe Chapman, Betty Compson, Ricardo Cortez, Viola Dana, Cecil B. De Mille, William de Mille, Charles De Roche, Dinky Dean, Helen Dunbar, Snitz Edwards, George Fawcett, Julia Faye, James Finlayson, Alec Francis, Jack Gardner, Sid Grauman, Alfred E. Green, Alan Hale, Lloyd Hamilton, Hope Hampton, William S. Hart, Gale Henry, Walter Hiers, Mrs. Walter Hiers, Stuart Holmes, Sigrid Holmquist, Jack Holt, Leatrice Joy, Mayme Kelso, J. Warren Kerrigan, Theodore Kosloff, Kosloff Dancers, Lila Lee, Lillian Leighton, Jacqueline Logan, May McAvoy, Robert McKim, Jeanie Macpherson, Hank Mann, Joe Martin, Thomas Meighan, Bull Montana, Owen Moore, Nita Naldi, Pola Negri, Anna Q. Nilsson, Charles Ogle, Guy Oliver, Kalla Pasha, Eileen Percy, Carmen Phillips, Jack Pickford, Chuck Reisner, Fritzi Ridgeway, Will Rogers, Sennett Girls, Ford Sterling, Anita Stewart, George Stewart, Gloria Swanson, Estelle Taylor, Ben Turpin, Bryant Washburn, Maude Wayne, Claire West, Laurence Wheat, Lois Wilson.

Synopsis

Angela Whitaker and her grandfather Joel visit Hollywood—the grandfather to regain his health and Angela to get into the movies. But Joel gets the offers. Then Angela's sweetheart Lem and the rest of Angela's family, hearing of grandfather Joel's debut, come to Hollywood to rescue him from "evil influences" and find themselves drawn into the movies.

Angela's ambitions wane after she marries Lem and gives birth to twins, who also show up on the silver screen. Angela and her family meet a number of screen celebrities.

Review

Seeing yourself as others see you is said to be good medicine. Showing yourself as others might see you if they had a six-cylinder sense of humor certainly is good fun. James Cruze has tried the latter experiment in *Hollywood*, made from a story by Frank Condon originally published in *Photoplay,* and the result is one of the most successful of Paramount pictures. All the motion picture people you ever heard of are in this picture. By laughing at himself and his crowd, Mr. Cruze has turned out a rattling good film.

    —*Photoplay,* October 1923.

The Cheat

96. Jack Holt, Negri. *The Cheat*, 1923.

Released September 30, 1923. Famous Players–Lasky Corporation.
Distribution: Paramount Pictures. 8 reels (7,323 feet).
Director: George Fitzmaurice.
Producer: Adolph Zukor, George Fitzmaurice.
Writers: Ouida Bergère, Hector Turnbull (story).
Cinematography: Arthur C. Miller.

Cast

Pola Negri (Carmelita De Córdoba), Jack Holt (Dudley Drake), Charles De Roche (Claude Mace/Prince Rao-Singh), Dorothy Cumming (Lucy Hodge), Robert Schable (Jack Hodge), Charles Stevenson (Horace Drake), Helen Dunbar (Duenna), Richard Wayne (Attorney for defense), Guy Oliver (District Attorney), Edward Kimball (Judge).

97. *The Cheat*, 1923. Pola Negri, Charles De Roche.

Synopsis

South American beauty Carmelita De Córdoba elopes with New York broker Dudley Drake, is disinherited by her father, and falls into the clutches of Prince Rao-Singh, a crook posing as an Indian prince. Carmelita tries to repay her debt to the prince; he refuses her check, and brands her as a cheat with his family crest. She shoots him, and then escapes. Dudley arrives and takes the rap, but he is acquitted when Carmelita shows the brand on her shoulder. The courtroom mobs the bogus prince.

Reviews

When it overcomes a slow start with cabarets and fashion displays and gets down to business, the picture becomes convincing and absorbing. Pola Negri is glorious in looks and acting but there is nothing inspired about Fitzmaurice's direction, considering the material he had to work with. It is, however, a mighty fine entertainment, just missing being a big picture.

—*Photoplay*, November 1923

The Cheat was a remake of Cecil B. DeMille's 1915 classic.

According to *Variety*, George Fitzmaurice walked off the film halfway through the production; Frank O'Connor completed it, by arrangement with Lasky.

Another mark for Paramount so far as production is concerned, but it doesn't mean a thing for the star. Pola Negri fails to convince in her characterization of a South American heiress ... and while the lavish interiors impress and the clothes of Miss Negri make the women talk, it doesn't alter the fact that a Monday night audience at the Rivoli laughed at it. Miss Negri throws upon the screen a distinctively hard personality, which, when she is vamping, is foolproof, but when it should create pathos, there is a direful lack that in roles of this sort is courting disaster.

—*Variety*, August 30, 1923

Here I am doing what I've always considered hopelessly dumb—writing to a fan magazine—but I feel that this particular column ["What the Fans Think"] of *Picture Play* is becoming increasingly valuable to the star, the producer, and to the public ... The case of Pola is the most striking. "Bella Donna" was fair, but "The Cheat"—words can't describe my feelings on seeing that. Of all the absurd, overdressed, disgusting exhibitions of bad taste, this picture gets the doormat. Is the fact that she made a great many poor pictures before coming to this country to be used as an excuse for the first two which were made over here?"

—Letter from a fan (Edward Seay, Los Angeles) in *Picture Play*, January 1924

Not a single word of quality—dull and asinine.

—*Motion Picture Magazine*, December 1923

The Spanish Dancer

98. *The Spanish Dancer*, 1923.

Released November 4, 1923. Famous Players–Lasky Corporation.

Distribution: Paramount Pictures.

Director: Herbert Brenon.

Producers: Adolph Zukor, Herbert Brenon.

Play: Philippe François Pinel, Adolphe Philippe d'Ennery.

Writer: June Mathis.

Cinematography: James Wong Howe (as James Howe).

Costumes: Howard Greer, André Lenoi Valasquez.

Cast

Pola Negri (Maritana, a Gypsy dancer), Antonio Moreno (Don César de Bazan), Wallace Beery (King Philip IV), Kathlyn Williams (Queen Isabel of Bourbon), Gareth Hughes (Lazarillo, a prisoner), Adolphe Menjou (Don Salluste, a courtier), Edward Kipling (Marquis de Rotundo), Anne Shirley as Dawn O'Day (Don Balthazar Carlos), Charles A. Stevenson

(Cardinal's ambassador), Robert Agnew (Juan, a thief), Buck Black (uncredited), Robert Brower (uncredited), Frank Coghlan Jr. (uncredited), Gino Corrado (uncredited), Johnny George (uncredited), Binunsky Hyman (uncredited), Boyd Irwin (uncredited), André Lenoi (uncredited), George J. Lewis (uncredited), Virginia Moon (Grandmother—uncredited), Lon Poff (uncredited), Henry Vogel (uncredited).

Edna Harron doubled for Miss Negri's dancing.

Virginia Moon had been a spy in the Civil War.

Synopsis

Maritana is in love with Don César, who is arrested and sentenced to die for dueling while assisting the youth Lazarillo, who had been beaten by the captain of the guards. Maritana seeks help from the queen, who requests that the king pardon Don César. Don César and Maritana are married. The king makes advances on Maritana. Don César breaks free from jail and saves her. The Queen arrives, jealous now, as the king and Don César battle. It is Maritana's quick wit which saves the king's reputation, and he rewards Don César by restoring him his estates.

Reviews

After being wasted in *Bella Donna* and *The Cheat*, Pola Negri comes back to her own in this picture. She is again La Negri of *Passion*. She has shed the veneer of sophistication and has reverted to the primitive woman type. As the gypsy girl in this adaptation of "Don Ceśar de Bazan," she gives a magnificent performance. She portrays almost every emotion conceivable and does each one admirably.

> —*Photoplay*, December 1923

Seeing the picture is like walking into a large family dinner party. You meet so many people that you get all confused and you forget who is related to whom. Somewhere in the big scenes is Pola Negri. She is a little less sleek and a little more spontaneous than she was in *The Cheat*. But she has lost something of her old surety and her audacity. Poor Pola! She should have had a studio and a studio staff all to herself.

> —*Picture Play*, January 1924

To Miss Pickford: In this department you recently gave your reasons for making *Rosita.* Is this not an unconscious admission of failure? Your work in *Rosita* is no more great than the dramatic merit of your former stories has been great. If Pola Negri had been given your cast and settings what would, and could she not have done with them? Her *Spanish Dancer* failed because it lacked all that you in such measure had.

—Letter from a fan (Mary E. Dreyman, New York) *in Picture Play,* February 1924

Shadows of Paris

99. Charles De Roche, Negri in *Shadows of Paris*, 1924.

Released February 17, 1924. Famous Players–Lasky Corporation.

Distribution: Paramount Pictures. 7 reels.

Director: Herbert Brenon.

Producers: Adolph Zukor, Jesse L. Lasky.

Writers: Eve Unsell, Fred Jackson.

Cinematography: Bert Baldridge.

Cast

Pola Negri (Claire, Queen of the Apaches), Charles De Roche (Fernand, an Apache), Huntley Gordon (Raoul, Minister of the Interior), Adolphe Menjou (Georges de Croy, his secretary), Gareth Hughes (Émile Boule), Vera Reynolds (Liane), Rose Dione (Madame Boule, café owner), Rosita Marstini (Madame Vali, a poetess), Edward Kipling (Pierre, a roué), Maurice Cannon (Robert, a taxi driver), Frank Nelson (Le Bossu, the hunchback), George O'Brien (Louis).

Synopsis

Claire, queen of the Paris underground, has risen to high society. Believing her lover Fernand is dead, she falls in love with Raoul. Raoul's secretary, de Croy, threatens Claire with her past in order to have her. Fernand returns and Claire no longer loves him. When attempting to steal a necklace, he is killed by de Croy, who has come to Claire's boudoir to collect his debt. Raoul returns during all of this, and de Croy keeps Claire's secret, stating he killed a thief stealing her jewels. Claire, however, confesses the truth. As she is about to leave, Raoul forgives her.

Reviews

Pola Negri as an Apache girl, the queen of a notorious café in Paris at the time of the World War. The role is a congenial one for Miss Negri and, as a result, the picture is much more satisfactory than some of her earlier ones. She is excellent as the Apache and as the wife of the Prefect of Police. Well directed with good atmosphere. Well worth seeing.
　—*Photoplay*, June 1924

When I see Pola Negri in such slush and remember her Carmen and her DuBarry, I could cry without calling for my glycerine. It's a shame, that's what it is. Yes, I am worked up over it. I, as a fair-minded reviewer, had to sit through all six reels—it seemed like twelve. You can walk out on it if you want to.
　—Martin Dickstein, *Screenland*, June 1924

Men

100. *Men*, 1924.

Released May 26, 1924. Famous Players–Lasky Corporation.

Distribution: Paramount Pictures. 7 reels.

Director: Dimitri Buchowetzki.

Producers: Adolph Zukor, Jesse L. Lasky.

Writers: Paul Bern (adaptation), Dimitri Buchowetzki.

Cinematography: Alvin Wyckoff.

Art Direction: Hans Dreier.

Cast

Pola Negri (Cleo), Robert Frazer (Georges Kleber), Robert Edeson (Henri Duval), Joseph Swickard (Cleo's father), Monte Collins (François), Gino Corrado (Stranger), Edgar Norton (Baron).

Synopsis

Cleo, a waitress in a Marseilles waterfront café, is lured to Paris by a baron, who betrays her. She resolves to use men to attain a life of luxury. After achieving acclaim and comfort as an entertainer, she meets Georges, a poor youth whose honesty in love restores her faith in men.

Reviews

The fiery, heavy-lidded Pola of *Passion* is back. In this story, written and directed by Dimitri Buchowetzki, there is the passionate, bitter cynicism that becomes her so well, and while the story is a little trashy and its treatment a little threadbare, it will entertain you if you are a Pola Negri fan.
    —*Photoplay*, July 1924

Pola Negri is the star, with three members featured. What reason there was for the featuring is a question, for Pola Negri in her last couple pictures has shown herself to be one of the real drawing cards of those working under the Paramount banner. In addition, this picture, according to the advance tip-off, was supposed to have been one of the best that she has done. That cannot truthfully be said, but it is a picture the fans are going to flock to see and like immensely.

'Tis a pretty tale; but there is more in the telling than the mere language. It is in the direction of Buchowetzki and the acting of Pola that make it.

Atmosphere! There's tons of it all over the place. Sets that are extremely flashy and a carnival scene that carries a real punch and carnival touch … And if Famous Players holds on to Buchowetzki they are going to find a distinct acquisition to their directorial staff.
    —*Variety*, May 7, 1924

Lily of the Dust

101. *Lily of the Dust*, 1924. Negri, Raymond Griffith.

Released August 24, 1924. Famous Players–Lasky Corporation.

Distribution: Paramount Pictures. 7 reels.

Director: Dimitri Buchowetzki.

Producers: Adolph Zukor, Jesse L. Lasky.

Writers: Paul Bern, Edward Sheldon (play—*Song of Songs*), Hermann Sudermann (novel—*Song of Songs*).

Cinematography: Alvin Wyckoff.

Art Direction: Hans Dreier.

Cast

Pola Negri (Lily Czepanek), Ben Lyon (Richard von Prell), Noah Beery (Colonel von Mertzbach), Raymond Griffith (Karl Dehnecke), Jeanette Daudet (Julia), William J. Kelly (Walter von Prell).

Synopsis

While working in a bookstore Lily meets Prell, a young German officer, who falls in love with her; but the "old man," Mertzbach, hears about her and takes her for his own wife. Finding Lily in the arms of Prell, Mertzbach wounds him in a duel and turns her out. She then accepts the attentions of Dehnecke, and Prell overlooks her liaison; but his uncle refuses to accept her, and she returns to Dehnecke.

Reviews

As a whole … if they like Pola they will accept this, but story far too sophisticated for average audience liking. Star gives another excellent performance. Noah Beery outstanding as Pola's husband who finally throws her over. Ben Lyon, Mr. Hero and does pretty well. Raymond Griffith not the continental type. Badly miscast. Others unimportant. Indeed, the atmosphere and types play an important part in the production. The director knows his Continental Europe and its people and this is definitely shown in the picture. One shot may prove objectionable—a fade out showing Lily's body quite nude—which Beery fancies he sees through her clothing. It isn't necessary and may cause difficulty. You know how your people feel about Pola. She hasn't had any too much fine material in her recent productions and if they still like her they'll come in for this. You will have to depend entirely upon the star because while many know the famous Sudermann story it's a type of material which is difficult to exploit—that is if you really want to go into the story. Because Lily—well she's just Lily. What happens to her—what it's all about is what you can talk about—if you can talk.

    —*Film Daily*, September 7, 1924

Pola Negri is always wonderful. In my opinion she is the only one to portray life as it is. To make an audience forget the actress and remember only the character she is portraying. I can see a soul there that a director fails to bring to light. The result is a sadly disconnecting offering. I refer to "A Lily of the Dust" which I saw last night. The themes selected for her are not appropriate, and she is not placed in the correct moods and situations. I wonder whether she will ever have a director who has as much ability to direct as she has to perform. If Pola Negri ever does, we will have perfection in motion picture entertainment.

    —Letter from a fan (Bernadette LaCombe) in *Photoplay*, 1925 (month unknown)

Forbidden Paradise

102. Rod La Rocque, Negri in *Forbidden Paradise*, 1924.

Released November 24, 1924. Famous Players–Lasky Corporation.

Distribution: Paramount Pictures. 8 reels.

Director: Ernst Lubitsch.

Producers: Adolph Zukor, Jesse L. Lasky.

Writers: Agnes Christine Johnston, Hans Kraly, Lajos Biró (play), Menyhért Lengyel (play).

Cinematography: Charles Van Enger.

Art Direction: Hans Dreier.

Costumes: Howard Greer.

Cast

Pola Negri (The Czarina), Rod La Rocque (Alexei), Adolphe Menjou (Chancellor), Pauline Starke (Anna), Fred Malatesta (French Ambassador), Nick De Ruiz (General), Carrie Daumery (Lady-in-Waiting), Clark Gable (Soldier—uncredited), Carlton Griffin (Officer—uncredited), William Quinn (uncredited), Leo White (Driver—uncredited).

Synopsis

Alexei, a young officer, saves the Czarina of a small European kingdom from revolutionary conspirators and is rewarded with her love. Infatuated, he deserts his sweetheart, Anna, the Czarina's Lady-in-Waiting, only to discover that his Queen is far from true to him. Desperate, he joins the revolutionists and plots against her. The Czarina pleads that she loves only him and he swears no harm will befall her. Meantime the Chancellor nips the revolution in the bud, and the Czarina orders Alexei's arrest. But she causes herself such unhappiness in doing so that she releases him from prison, relinquishing him to Anna, and seeks solace in a new affair with the French Ambassador.

—*Exhibitor's Trade Review*, December 6, 1924

103. *Forbidden Paradise*, 1924. Negri, Rod La Rocque, Pauline Starke.

Reviews

One of the really great pictures of the year. Taken from the play "The Czarina," it forms itself, in the hands of a capable cast and director, into a demonstration of the best that can be done in motion pictures. It is a story of a queen who loved not wisely but too well. Pola Negri plays the queen and gives one of the finest, if not the finest, performances of her career. Ernst Lubitsch never gave a finer exhibition of directing than he did in this

Forbidden Paradise was remade in 1945 as *A Royal Scandal*, starring Tallulah Bankhead. Ernst Lubitsch was uncredited as director. The film's director was Otto Preminger.

picture. He has at his command all his old wizardry. May Pola always have him as her director and may he always have Pola to direct. The combination develops the best dramatic talents in both. If you like pictures of this description don't miss this film. Just a few more words about Pola's *Catherine.* She is what one might call a good bad woman. But her wickedness is done gorgeously and regally. And her goodly actions are done in humanly and womanly fashion. The combination cloaks her with a rare quality of diplomacy that leaves her always in command of any situation that arises. And that trait denotes genius.

—*Photoplay*, January 1925

In the play itself, Catherine the Great of Russia was the central figure. The period was of her day. In the film, Queen Catherine of an unnamed kingdom is the central figure and the time is today. That change in period worked no wrong in this case … and many bits of comedy were worked in which could never have been placed in a costume picture of several hundred years back [such as modern devices like the telephone—very reminiscent of the 1949 film *A Connecticut Yankee in King Arthur's Court*].

—*Variety*, November 1924

East of Suez

Pola Negri e Noah Beery
in " *All'ombra delle Pagode* "

104. *East of Suez*. Negri with Noah Beery. 1925.

Released January 12, 1925. Famous Players–Lasky Corporation.
Distribution: Paramount Pictures. 7 reels.
Director: Raoul Walsh.
Producers: Adolph Zukor, Jesse L. Lasky.
Writers: Sada Cowan, W. Somerset Maugham (story).
Cinematography: Victor Milner.
Art Direction: Hans Dreir.
Costume Design: Howard Greer (uncredited).

Cast

Pola Negri (Daisy Forbes), Edmund Lowe (George Tevis), Rockliffe Fellowes (Harry Anderson), Noah Beery (British Consul), Sojin (Lee Tai), Mrs. Wong Wing (Amah), Florence Regnart (Sylvia Knox), Charles Requa (Harold Knox), E.H. Calvert (Sidney Forbes), Jesse Fuller (uncredited).

Synopsis

After being educated in England, Daisy returns to China, the country of her birth, and discovers her father has died. She has become a social outcast, owing to the public revelation that the oriental nurse who raised her was in actuality her mother. In love with George, the nephew of the British Consul, Daisy is disappointed by him when he is persuaded by his uncle to renounce her in favor of a diplomatic career. Lee Tai, a sinister Mandarin, kidnaps and drugs Daisy; but she is rescued by Harry Anderson, a rotter whom she soon marries out of desperation. When Anderson discovers Daisy is an outcast, he bitterly regrets their marriage. George searches for Daisy, only to find her married. Anderson forbids George to see Daisy again, but George defies the ban and meets her at her house to bid farewell. Before he can shoot George, Anderson drinks poisoned wine from Lee Tai, and dies. George takes Daisy back to England, and Lee Tai is executed according to Chinese law.

Reviews

Something of a "come-down" for Pola Negri. On the stage Somerset Maugham's play carried a real dramatic flavor but in the screen version nothing even seems to develop. It is keyed in morbid pitch and the action becomes often commonplace. The highlights are found in the details and atmosphere—and Negri is always colorful.

    —*Motion Picture Magazine*, April 1925

East of Suez, the Somerset Maugham play that served Florence Reed so well on the stage, is a good vehicle for Pola Negri on the screen. As a matter of fact Miss Negri's performance is to be desired above that of Miss Reed, if anything. Miss Negri … proves she can troupe with a repression and still get over all the fire of dramatic intensity. Raoul Walsh has directed a picture that holds the attention from beginning to end with its suspense. The combination of Pola Negri, the title of the picture, and the strong cast should mean money to almost any box office anywhere.

    —*Variety*, January 7, 1925

The Charmer

105. Negri in *The Charmer*, 1925.

Released April 20, 1925. Famous Players–Lasky Corporation.

Distribution: Paramount Pictures. 6 reels.

Director: Sidney Olcott.

Producers: Adolph Zukor, Jesse L. Lasky.

Writer: Sada Cowan.

Cinematography: James Wong Howe (as James Howe).

Film Editor: Patricia Rooney.

Cast

Pola Negri (Mariposa), Wallace MacDonald (Ralph Bayne), Robert Frazer (Dan Murray), Trixie Friganza (Mama), Cesare Gravina (Señor Sprott), Gertrude Astor (Bertha Sedgwick), Edwards Davis (Mr. Sedgwick), Mathilda Brundage (Mrs. Bayne).

Synopsis

Mariposa, a wild dancer in a cheap Seville Café, is taken to New York by Sprott, a prominent theatrical producer. Billed as "The Charmer," she becomes the toast of two continents. Among her most ardent admirers are Ralph Bayne, a millionaire playboy, and his chauffeur, Dan Murray, both of whom first met her in Spain. Madly in love with Bayne, Mrs. Sedgwick invites Mariposa and her mother to a weekend party in a deliberate attempt to humiliate the dancer. Bayne quickly realizes that Mariposa is out of place in high society, and, determining to make her his mistress, takes her home with him. Mrs. Sedgwick unexpectedly arrives at Bayne's suite, closely followed by her suspicious husband, and Mariposa protects the society woman's reputation at the cost of her own. Murray arrives and attempts at gunpoint to force Bayne to marry Mariposa, but she objects and declares her intention of marrying Murray instead.

Reviews

Although the picture is off Negri's hunting ground, inasmuch as she does no vamping or sophisticated female stuff here, it demonstrates a versatility which extends to the playing of sweeter and more sympathetic roles ... *The Charmer* is excellent first run material, will fit any program and give entertainment. Just because it has Negri in a different sort of role—don't get frightened. Apparently the change is well advised.
  —*Variety*, April 8, 1925

Never does Pola Negri make a picture we do not breathe a fervent prayer that the direction of it will be placed in the capable hands of Ernst Lubitsch, for there were never a director and a star who worked in more perfect accord than do these two. As "Mariposa" she is loved by two men—a chauffeur and his wealthy employer, and one is undecided as to just where her affections are placed until the big scene in which Pola compromises herself to save another woman—a situation which has been in pictures once or twice before, and falls rather flat with the repetition. Unless you compare Pola's *Passion* with *The Charmer* you will probably enjoy the latter.
  —*Movie Weekly*, May 9, 1925

Flower of Night

106. *Flower of Night*, 1925. Negri with Helen Lee Worthing.

Released November 2, 1925. Famous Players–Lasky Corporation.

Distribution: Paramount Pictures. 7 reels.

Director: Paul Bern.

Producers: Adolph Zukor, Jessie L. Lasky.

Writers: Willis Goldbeck, Joseph Hergesheimer (story).

Cinematography: Bert Glennon.

Music: Clarke Lewis.

Cast

Pola Negri (Carlota y Villalon), Joseph Dowling (Don Geraldo y Villalon), Youcca Troubetzkoy (John Basset), Warner Oland (Luke Rand), Edwin J. Brady (Derck Bylandt), Eulalie Jensen (Mrs. Bylandt), Cesare Gravina (Servant), Gustav von Seyffertitz (Vigilante leader), Helen Lee Worthing (Josefa), Thais Valdemar, Manuel Acosta, Frankie Bailey.

Synopsis

California 1856: Don Geraldo has lost his gold mine to dishonest Americans. Carlota, his daughter, is in love with John Basset, the mine's new assistant superintendent. Against her father's wishes, she goes to a dance to see Basset. At the dance, Derck Bylandt, the superintendent, gets drunk, tries to force Carlota to dance with him, and then dies of a heart attack. Basset is disgusted, ignoring Carlota. Carlota confesses to her father she has disgraced the Villalon name and he commits suicide. She then goes to San Francisco and becomes a dance hall girl. There she accepts the offer of Luke Rand, the sinister head of the Vigilance Committee, to help her recover the mine. She recants when she realizes Basset's life is in danger. In the end, Basset kills Rand, and Carlota and Basset realize their mutual love.

Review

The combination of Negri and Hergesheimer should have produced at least a very worthwhile picture if not a masterpiece. Great things were expected, which makes the disappointment doubly keen after witnessing *Flower of Night*. It is difficult to obtain sympathy for the leading character as portrayed by Miss Negri because her introductory scenes stamp her as hard boiled and sophisticated. Consequently, many fine bits of acting which she contributes later in the story are ineffective. Pola's personal fans will enjoy bits of this picture, her dancing, for instance, but Mr. Bern, director, Mr. Goldbeck, scenarist, and Mr. Hergesheimer, author, you have made us lose faith in Santa Claus.

    —*Photoplay*, December 1925

A Woman of the World

107. Negri in *A Woman of the World*, 1925.

Released December 28, 1925. Famous Players–Lasky Corporation.

Distribution: Paramount Pictures.

Director: Malcolm St. Clair.

Producers: Adolph Zukor, Jesse L. Lasky.

Writers: Pierre Collings, Carl Van Vechten (story—*The Tattooed Countess*).

Cinematography: Bert Glennon.

Cast

Pola Negri (Countess Elnora Natatorini), Charles Emmett Mack (Gareth Johns), Holmes Herbert (Richard Granger), Blanche Mehaffey (Lennie Porter), Chester Conklin (Sam Poore), Lucille Ward (Lou Poore), Guy Oliver (Judge Porter), Dot Farley (Mrs. Baerbauer), May Foster (Mrs. Fox), Dorothea Wolbert (Annie), Marcelle Corday (guest).

Synopsis

The Countess, disappointed in love, leaves Europe and comes to America to stay with a cousin, Sam, who lives in a small Midwestern town. Her beauty and manner start much gossip and soon, such slanders are heard by Granger, the reforming and virtuous district attorney. He orders her to leave; she refuses. After Granger castigates her, she horse-whips him. Because he takes the beating with good grace, she realizes he is in love with her. Dropping the whip, they embrace while exchanging proposals and acceptances.

According to film historian Kevin Brownlow, *A Woman of the World* is "First rate!"

Reviews

Poor Pola! Wonder what they are trying to do to her, anyway? If something isn't done, then Pola Negri's value as a box-office attraction in the spots where that does exist is going to be wiped out. This picture is just another horrible example of what she should not do. It doesn't look as though it was going to be worth a nickel at the box office. Pola has a new bob, and it is the type that is not going to endear her, particularly to the women, evident through the comments made by women in the audience at the Rivoli at the final show Sunday night. Pola seemed to get on their nerves. It is just a small-time picture that that might have been turned out by any dink independent.

—*Variety*, December 16, 1925

Will somebody please find a story for Pola Negri? Not since *Forbidden Paradise* came out nearly a year ago has she had any worthwhile study in celluloid. If something isn't done quickly, her pictures are doomed and Pola, herself, will pass into an eclipse.

—*Motion Picture Magazine*, March 1926

The Crown of Lies

108. *The Crown of Lies*, 1926. Negri with Noah Beery.

Released April 12, 1926. Famous Players–Lasky Corporation.

Distribution: Paramount Pictures. 5 reels.

Director: Dimitri Buchowetski.

Producers: Adolph Zukor, Jesse L. Lasky.

Writers: Hope Loring, Louis D. Lighton, Ernest Vajda (story).

Cinematography: Bert Glennon.

Cast

Pola Negri (Olga Kriga), Noah Beery (Count Mirko), Robert Ames (John Knight), Charles A. Post (Karl), Arthur Hoyt (Fritz), Mikhael Vavitch (Vorski), Cissy FitzGerald (Leading Lady), May Foster (Landlady), Frankie Bailey (Actress), Edward Cecil (Leading Man), Erwin Connelly (Stage Manager).

Synopsis

Olga dreams of becoming a great actress but is turned down by the theater manager because of jealousy with his leading lady. So, she leaves with her admirer John, who has accepted a job offer in a small Balkan country. She meets Karl, an alien, who is convinced she is Queen of Sylvania and begs her to return with him. She does and is greeted by Count Mirko and his ministers. The Count formulates a plan to use Olga's deception for his own personal gain. She arrives in Sylvania with John where Vorski, a tyrant, agrees to pay for her removal. After a revolt, she ascends the throne and happiness is restored. She then returns to New York with John.

Reviews

When all is said and done there is nothing to the Ernest Vajda tale but a little rewrite on *Such a Little Queen*. It does, however, give Pola a chance to act regally, and after all maybe that's what Pola wanted to do ... Pola Negri does fairly well in the earlier comedy moments and then during the tragedy that leads up to her coming on the throne is queenly enough, but she does all of the latter with a certain matter-of-factness that isn't at all imposing. *The Crown of Lies* isn't one of those pictures that anyone is going to rave about and is classified as any ordinary program picture.

> —*Variety*, April 7, 1926

Poor Pola, she has our sympathy. About two more pictures like this and as far as the movie public is concerned, she will be through. It may not be her fault, unless she insists on the impossible vehicles she travels in. Pola is still as interesting and as beautiful as ever and we are anxiously looking forward to the proposed combination of Von Stroheim and Pola. Yes, sir, we'll bet that will be a picture.

> —*Photoplay*, June 1926

Good and Naughty

109. *Good and Naughty,* 1926. Negri with Tom Moore.

Released June 7, 1926. Famous Players–Lasky Corporation.

Distribution: Paramount Pictures. 6 reels.

Director: Malcolm St. Clair.

Producers: Adolph Zukor, Jesse L. Lasky.

Writers: Pierre Collings, Henry Falk (play), René Peter (play).

Cinematography: Bert Glennon.

Costumes: Howard Greer (uncredited).

Cast

Pola Negri (Germaine Morris), Tom Moore (Gerald Gray), Ford Sterling (Bunny West), Miss Du Pont (Claire Fenton), Stuart Holmes (Thomas Fenton), Marie Mosquini (Chouchou Rouselle), Warner Richmond ("Bad News" Smith).

Synopsis

Germaine is in love with her employer Gerald Gray, an interior decorator who is concerned over his affair with Claire Fenton, the wife of a wealthy broker. Claire invites Gerald on a yachting trip, and Gerald's friend Bunny invites showgirl Chouchou to pose as Gerald's fiancée. Germaine, however, decides to substitute herself and in Florida she wins the attentions of all the men; thus develops a quarrel between Claire and Gerald. Thomas, Claire's husband, hopes to obtain a divorce. Germaine, in her negligee, delivers a pipe to Gerald's room; he proposes. Thomas suggests that Gerald take Germaine, leaving Claire to go her own way. However, Smith tries to claim Germaine and is beaten by Gerald, who succeeds in reconciling the Fentons while claiming the girl he loves.

Reviews

Every other director on the Lasky lot has been assigned to direct Pola Negri—so it was quite to be expected that Mal St. Clair would have his opportunity of trying to make a worthy picture with her. He has succeeded where others have failed. The result is a brisk little hodge-podge of comedy and fine manners... But St. Clair has brought forth Pola as a comedienne, and that is the big achievement of the picture. The public has almost despaired of seeing the star in a story that fits her histrionic stature. *Good and Naughty* is Pola's best American film.

—*Motion Picture Magazine*, September 1926

In a measure Pola gets a chance to act, to do something other than look beautiful. That is in the earlier portion of the picture when she is posing as a slovenly assistant in the interior decorator's shop. Pola does several things here that make her really worthwhile. There is a repression about her work that proves she is an artiste who when given the chance can score without clothes.

—*Variety*, June 16, 1926

Why do the producers import foreign talent? The importation started, and should have ended, with Pola Negri. Since coming to this country she has shown only occasional flashes to incite interest in her. Except for making the front page with marvelous regularity she has most emphatically failed to justify the high hopes we had for her. The smouldering genius of *Passion* is no more... Let's give the home girls a chance, let Germany, Sweden, Poland, and the Lord knows where else have their respective Mary Pickfords AND pay their salaries. If we must be high-hatted, let it be by Americans!

—Letter from a filmgoer (Constance Schank, Kersey, Colorado) in *Photoplay*, May 1926

Hotel Imperial

110. Negri in *Hotel Imperial*, 1927.

Released February 26, 1927. Famous Players–Lasky Corporation.

Distribution: Paramount Pictures. 8 reels.

Director: Mauritz Stiller.

Producers: Adolph Zukor, Jesse L. Lasky, Erich Pommer.

Writers: Jules Furthman (screenplay), Lajos Biró (story), Edwin Justus Mayer (titles), E. Lloyd Sheldon (editing).

Costumes: Howard Greer (uncredited).

Cinematography: Bert Glennon.

Cast

Pola Negri (Anna Sedlak), James Hall (Paul Almasy), George Siegmann (General Juschkiewitsch), Max Davidson (Elias Butterman), Michael Vavitch (Tabakowitsch), Otto Fries (Anton Klinak), Nicholas Soussanin (Baron Fredrikson), Golden Wadhams (Major General Sultanov), Joseph Swickard (Austrian General—uncredited); Adrienne Ames, stand-in for Negri.

Synopsis

Six Hungarian Hussars, weary from fighting, ride into a frontier town and discover it occupied by the Russians. The lieutenant, Paul, drags himself to the porter's lodge of the Hotel Imperial where he falls asleep. Anna, Elias, and Anton, three remaining servants, carry him to a bedroom, and the next morning Anna persuades him to pose as a waiter. Anna is courted by General Juschkiewitsch, whose advances she accepts in order to secure Paul's safety. Tabakowitsch, a spy, returns from the front and learns Paul has plans which may rout Hungarian forces. Paul kills him but Anna comes to his defense. The Hungarians reclaim their town and Anna and Paul are reunited.

Remade in 1939 as *Hotel Imperial* with Isa Miranda, directed by Robert Florey; and again in 1943 as *Five Graves to Cairo* with Anne Baxter, directed by Billy Wilder.

Reviews

Just another war picture. Great things were expected of the combination of Mauritz Stiller, Erich Pommer, [and] Pola Negri, but the result is just a program picture. In direction and camera work the picture stands out, but the story isn't one that is going to give anyone a great thrill. Stiller and Pommer have done their work well, and they have made Pola look like a gorgeous beauty in some shots, and effectively handled her in others…but to what avail is good direction and supervision plus acting, when the story isn't there?
　　—*Variety*, January 25, 1927

Erich Pommer, that intrepid German producer, has made, through the excellent direction of Mauritz Stiller, a very great picture. It accomplishes almost to perfection those photographic effects which directors have been striving for. Pola Negri does her best work since coming to America. It is a smooth, eloquent tale told in an entirely new language—a thrilling language of pictures. It is almost altogether a story of the reaction of individuals to war. Don't miss this great picture.
　　—*Motion Picture Magazine*, January 1927

Barbed Wire

Released September 10, 1927. Paramount Famous Lasky Corporation.

Distribution: Paramount Pictures. 7 reels.

Directors: Rowland V. Lee, Mauritz Stiller (uncredited).

Producers: Adolph Zukor, Jesse. L. Lasky, Erich Pommer (uncredited), B. P. Schulberg, Rowland V. Lee (uncredited).

Writers: Hall Caine (novel—*The Woman of Knockaloe*), Rowland V. Lee (adaptation), Jules Furthman (screenplay).

Cinematography: Bert Glennon.

Editing: E. Lloyd Sheldon.

Art director: Hans Dreier.

Technical director: Louis Van der Ecker (uncredited).

Costumes: Travis Banton (uncredited), Edith Head.

Knockaloe was a camp for aliens (non-citizens) on the Isle of Man.

Cast

Pola Negri (Mona), Clive Brook (Oskar), Claude Gillingwater (Jean Moreau), Einar Hanson (André Moreau), Clyde Cook (Hans), Gustav von Seyffertitz (Pierre Corlet), Charles Lane (Colonel Duval), Ben Hendricks Jr. (Sergeant Caron).

Synopsis

Normandy, 1914. War has broken out. Mona, a peasant girl is left to take care of the farm for her father and brother. The farm is confiscated by the French authorities for a prison camp. Although she despises Germans, Mona becomes attracted to Oskar, a young prisoner working the farm. A French sergeant attempts to break into Mona's house, but Oskar comes to her aid and is charged with assault. She is branded a traitor at his trial. After the Armistice, the camp is ordered cleared, but the villagers refuse to harbor the boy. Mona's blinded brother returns from the war and shames the people with an impassioned plea for love and forgiveness.

Reviews

War, intercollegiate sports, and cabarets are the three themes absorbing Hollywood right now. The movie moguls pronounce them sure-fire and box-office. Pola Negri's newest, *Barbed Wire*, is, naturally enough, a story of the World War. Like her last film, *Hotel Imperial*, it is an excellent photoplay. These are her first two effective screen vehicles in a long line of inferior celluloid. The picture, frequently turgid and heavily sentimental, has many moving and even thrilling moments. Miss Negri never has been better than as the peasant girl torn between love and patriotism.

—*Liberty Magazine*, October 1, 1927

Pola Negri's commanding presence dominates, because she is scarcely ever off the screen, but she does not suggest the emotional peasant. She is more the calculating actress—as well as an accomplished one, particularly in a gripping scene where she is cheered and acclaimed by the German soldiers for saving one of their number from death.

—*Picture Play*, November 1927

I heartily agree with Irene Hart about John Gilbert and would like to add the name of Pola Negri, who appears to have babbled to every press man in the five continents. There is still a certain not-inconsiderable section of the public which, without knowing anything about them, looks down on all film people as a weird and wonderful collection of people who ought to have a zoo to themselves. Such critics are to be strongly condemned, but people like Gilbert, who informs the world with great gusto that Greta Garbo is the most wonderful girl on earth, or like Negri, who announces that she has—for the fourth or fifth time—found the greatest love of her life, do more harm than anything else toward increasing criticism of the movie people. There are two little proverbs which the two stars mentioned might bear in mind. One is that still waters run deep, and the other, that empty barrels make the most noise.

—Letter from a filmgoer (Constance K. Ridley, London, England) in *Picture Play*, November 1927

The Woman on Trial

Released October 29, 1927. Paramount Famous Lasky Corporation.

Distribution: Paramount Famous Lasky Corporation.

Director: Mauritz Stiller.

Producer: B. P. Schulberg.

Writers: Elsie von Koczain, Julian Johnson (titles),

Hope Loring (adaptation), Ernest Vajda (play—*Confession*).

Cinematography: Bert Glennon.

Costumes: Travis Banton (uncredited).

Cast

Pola Negri (Julie), Einar Hanson (Pierre Bouton), Arnold Kent (Gaston Napier), André Sarti (John Morland), Baby Dorothy Brock (Paul), Valentina Zimina (Henrietta), Sidney Bracy (Brideaux), Bertram Marburgh (Morland's lawyer), Gayne Whitman (Julie's lawyer), Oscar Beregi, Sr.

> Actor Ricardo Cortez walked off the set of *The Woman on Trial* and was replaced by Einar Hanson.

Synopsis

Julie, on trial for the murder of Gaston, recalls the events of her life six years earlier: She is in love with Pierre, an artist who is sickly. At a party at Gaston's, she prevents Pierre's suicide. Julie meets John Morland, a wealthy suitor who again makes her a marriage offer. She accepts, thinking this will allow her to obtain money to care for Pierre. Five years later, John's jealousy drives Julie to seek consolation in her only child, Paul. John finds a letter from Pierre who is convalescing at a sanitarium. Learning Julie has visited him there, Morland forbids her to see her son. Julie kidnaps the child and a divorce results in the child staying with his mother. Morland forces Gaston, who owes John money, to arrange a compromising situation in his studio. Julie realizes the cruel trickery and shoots Gaston. She is acquitted and leaves with her son Paul, ultimately finding happiness with Pierre.

Reviews

One is rather startled as *The Woman on Trial* progresses to find the flaming, sophisticated Pola Negri carrying on in the role of a persecuted mother, given to tender broodings over her child. How the fans will adjust themselves to this violent innovation is a question. The quality of the play in which this usually vivid actress is concerned here doesn't help a pretty difficult situation. It is thoroughly theatrical and strangely alien in tone and locale. Such is the gushy history that is laboriously and ponderously unfolded in settings … and played out painstakingly by capable actors, who must have known at the time that this sort of sentimental slush was futile.

> —*Variety*, September 28, 1927

To Director Mauritz Stiller goes the glory of this extraordinarily fine film. His compelling, vivid treatment turns a melodramatic story into a penetrating character study of a woman and the three men in her life. Not for the children but for all adults interested in better movies.

> —*Photoplay*, August 1927

One letter in "What the Fans Think" department amused me. It spoke of the "fiery Pola" and the "inane, helpless" Lillian. The last time I saw Pola Negri, in "The Woman on Trial," she was far from fiery. In fact, she did a poor imitation of Lillian Gish. My idea of fiery acting is that given by Gloria Swanson in "Sadie Thompson." Pola is sunk too deep in sables and luxury to have much fire left.

> —Letter from a filmgoer (E.E., Germantown, Pennsylvania) in *Picture Play*, July 1928

The Secret Hour

111. *The Secret Hour*, 1928. Kenneth Thomson, Rowland V. Lee, Negri, Jean Hersholt.

Released February 4, 1928. Paramount Famous Lasky Corporation.

Distribution: Paramount Famous Lasky Corporation. 8 reels.

Director: Rowland V. Lee.

Producers: Adolph Zukor, Jesse L. Lasky.

Writers: Sidney Howard (play—*They Knew What They Wanted*), Julian Johnson (titles), Rowland V. Lee.

Cinematography: Harry Fischbeck.

Editing: Robert Bassler.

Cast

Pola Negri (Amy), Jean Hersholt (Tony), Kenneth Thomson (Joe), Christian J. Frank (Sam), George Kuwa (Ah Gee), George Periolat (Doctor).

Synopsis

Tiring of bachelorhood, Tony, an elderly gent, sends a photo of his foreman, Joe, to capture the heart of an attractive waitress, Amy. She falls in love with the photo. Meanwhile, Tony has an auto accident preventing him from meeting Amy's train. He sends Joe instead. Joe and Amy have an instant magnetism and secretly marry, regretting their decision the next morning. Three months later and able to walk again, Tony plans to marry Amy but when they tell him their secret, he orders them out of the house. He later relents and forgives them, realizing he was at fault for substituting Joe's photograph.

Reviews

Far from among her best pictures, *The Secret Hour* is not among Pola Negri's least. Faced with the problem of converting the highly censorable play of *They Knew What They Wanted* into celluloid pablum for innocents, those concerned in the task tackled a stiff job. Miss Negri plays with careful restraint unlighted by any sparks. So completely is she in character, she never once gives any hint that she has known the ermine of royalty.
—*Picture Play*, June 1928

Paramount has become the "killer" of stars—and their worst crime has been the killing of Pola Negri as a star. Recently I noticed a beautiful front page picture of Pola in a newspaper. The accompanying news item explained that upon the expiration of Miss Negri's contract, Paramount will not renew it, due to the fact that lately she has not been the drawing card of her early American years. Also, this would place her in the ranks of the has-beens. To Paramount I would say, is it any wonder your stars "die," when you consider the screen material given them? Paramount was too busy bringing trivial players to public notice, so, naturally, we saw a great deal of such players, and their reliable talent had to take a back seat. This is dangerous and most unfortunate for any star, but to think that the star of *Passion* and *Gypsy Blood* should meet with such a fate is outrageous.
—Letter from a fan (Carl L., Edinboro, Pennsylvania) in *Picture Play*, March 1928

Three Sinners

112. Negri in *Three Sinners*. 1928.

Released April 14, 1928. Paramount Famous Lasky Corporation.

Distribution: Paramount Famous Lasky Corporation. 8 reels.

Director: Rowland V. Lee.

Producers: Jesse L. Lasky, Rowland V. Lee, Adolph Zukor.

Production management: B. P. Schulberg

Writers: Rudolf Österreicher and Rudolph Bernauer (play—*Das zweite Leben*), Doris Anderson (adaptation), Jean de Limur (adaptation), Julian Johnson (titles), Rudolph Bernauer (play).

Cinematography: Victor Milner.

Film editing: Robert Bassler.

Costumes: Travis Banton, Eugene Joseff (uncredited—jewelry).

Cast

Pola Negri (Baroness Gerda Wallentin), Warner Baxter (James Harris), Paul Lukas (Count Dietrich Wallentin), Anders Randolph (Count Hellemuth Wallentin), Tullio Carminati (Raoul Stanislav), Anton Vaverka (Valet to Dietrich), Ivy Harris (Countess Lilli), William von Hardenburg (Prince von Scherson), Olga Baclanova (Baroness Hilda Brings), Robert Klein (Count Bogumil Sdarschinsky), Irving Bacon (uncredited), Delmer Daves (uncredited).

Synopsis

Perceiving that her husband no longer loves her, Gerda agrees to leave for Vienna, leaving her husband to pursue his political ambitions with Baroness Brings. While traveling, Gerda is seduced by Raoul and she leaves the train for a while. Later, she discovers that the train has crashed, killing everyone. Gerda feels guilt about her affair and does not notify her husband she has survived and is alive. Somewhat later, as hostess in a gambling den, she sees her husband who is strangely attracted to her. She discloses her identity and returns with her husband. Later, seeing that he does not really love her, she takes their child and sails to America with a wealthy patron of the gambling house.

Reviews

Pretty thin material for an hour's film running. Magnificent physical production, but another story which offers Pola Negri a pale story for her vivid type of acting … The principal appeal of the picture for women is that it furnishes Negri with opportunity to wear some stunning clothes and appear in a white wig, which makes her more beautiful than any disguise she has lately assumed. The production has to make its way on these grounds, for its story is without punch, develops in leisurely style, and is loosely woven. It was probably picked because it seemed appropriate to put Miss Negri back in the atmosphere of Continental polite society, in which she first came before the American public, surroundings to which this exotic actress properly belongs.

> —*Variety*, April 25, 1928

This is heavy drama, adroitly handled and exceptionally well acted. A Pola Negri picture which should satisfy her European following and intrigue American audiences. Pola metamorphoses from a drab, everyday wife of a German nobleman to a scintillating, fascinating woman of the world through the penalty she is forced to pay for one night of sin. She is as uninteresting in the first role as she is ravishing in the second.

> —*Photoplay*, June, 1928

Loves of an Actress

113. *Loves of an Actress*, 1928. Paul Lukas, Pola Negri.

Released August 18, 1928. Paramount Famous Lasky Corporation.

Distribution: Paramount Famous Lasky Corporation. 8 reels.

Director: Rowland V. Lee.

Producers: Adolph Zukor, Jesse L. Lasky.

Writers: Baroness von Hutten (book), Ernest Vajda (story), Julian Johnson (titles), Rowland V. Lee.

Cinematography: Victor Milner.

Editing: Robert Bassler, E. Lloyd Sheldon.

Music: Karl Hajos.

Cast

Pola Negri (Rachel), Nils Asther (Raoul Duval), Mary McAllister (Lisette), Richard Tucker (Baron Hartman), Philip Strange (Count Vareski), Paul Lukas (Dr. Durande), Nigel De Brulier (Count Morency), Helene Giere (Marie), Dean Harrell.

Synopsis

Born into a family of poor peasants, Rachel becomes a leading actress in the Comédie Française via three men: Baron Hartman, the wealthiest man in France, Count Vareski, relative of Napolean, and Dr. Durand, the leading newspaper publisher in Europe. All three men are in love with her, but she throws them over for Raoul Duval, soon to be appointed ambassador to Russia. The doctor threatens to publish Rachel's love letters to Raoul. To protect Raoul's reputation, Rachel pretends that she has only been toying with his emotions. Raoul goes to Russia, and Rachel, exhausted by life and love, peacefully dies.

Review

This is Pola Negri's last picture for Paramount. But Pola is almost completely lost sight of in the general turmoil of the film. Those sound effects so dear to Paramount drown her out. Especially, as she is not permitted to speak a word. Pola and her beau ride along on a coach, and the clop, clop of the horses is distinctly audible, but the lovers are allowed to coo in complete silence. In the theater scenes, the clamor of the stage door Johnnies is loud, but Pola dismisses them with lips that open and shut noiselessly. Also, the first baby to squall in photophone does so in this picture. General uproar and small assorted noises are plentiful, but no dialogue is spoken. And the cast is full of famous names. But to no avail. They just clutter up the sets like a flock of professional whoopee makers.

    —*Motion Picture Magazine*, November 1928

The Woman from Moscow

Released November 3, 1928. Paramount Famous Lasky Corporation.

Distribution: Paramount Famous Lasky Corporation. 7 reels.

Director: Ludwig Berger.

Producers: Ludwig Berger, Jesse L. Lasky, Adolph Zukor.

Production management: B. P. Schulberg.

Writers: Victorien Sardou (play—*Fedora*), John Farrow (screenplay, titles).

Cinematography: Victor Milner.

Editing: Frances Marsh, E. Lloyd Sheldon.

Music: Karl Hajos.

Cast

Pola Negri (Princess Fedora), Norman Kerry (Loris Ipanoff), Paul Lukas (Vladimir), H. B. Warner (Col. Stradimirovitsch), Otto Matiesen (Gretch Milner), Maude George (Olga Andreavitshka), Bodil Rosing (Nadia), Jack Luden (Ipanoff's brother), Martha Franklin (Ipanoff's mother), Mirra Rayo (Ipanoff's sister), Tetsu Komai (Groom).

Synopsis

When Princess Fedora's fiancé, Vladimir, is found murdered, she sets out to find Loris Ipanoff, whom she suspects of killing him. When she meets Loris, not knowing who he is, she falls in love with him. When she discovers his true identity she believes him innocent of the murder. However, Loris confesses to the murder and Fedora betrays him to Vladimir's father. She then discovers that Loris killed Vladimir in self-defense and she protects him against the assassins hired by Vladimir's father. Loris's family is ordered to Siberia and he turns against Fedora. She takes poison. Contrite, Loris returns to Fedora, in time to hold her in his arms as she dies.

Reviews

Pola Negri gives beauty and dignity to *The Woman from Moscow*, her last picture for Paramount. Those who have remained loyal throughout the fluctuations of her career in Hollywood will recognize this. Other, more casual filmgoers may find Pola's farewell heavy and the picture dull. I did neither. True, the story of *Fedora*, on which the picture is based, was written in 1882 and is therefore not of this age; but that does not make it less effective a medium for Pola's talent—a talent above and beyond that required by *Our Dancing Daughters*, or any of the so-called modern stories.

—*Picture Play*, February 1929

BACLANOVA! What a thrill the listener receives at the mere mention of this famous name... But poor Pola! And we are to see her no more? Oh, what a foolish thing is happening. Pola, the artist I have been praising and whose pictures I have never missed, is to be with us no more. Please let her stay. One-fourth of the best entertainment in the movies comes from her pictures. She and Baclanova combined will give us some rare entertainment. Why ship her off when we have so many other minor talented actresses who are raking in huge salaries every week while an artist of rare caliber has to give up her throne. My head will never lie easy until Pola comes back. I am keeping the photo she sent me as a memento of the best pictures I have enjoyed in my life.

—Letter from a fan (Albert Manski, Webster, Massachusetts) in *Motion Picture Magazine*, November 1928

A Woman Commands

114. *A Woman Commands*, 1932. Negri, Basil Rathbone.

Released January 1, 1932. RKO Radio Pictures, Inc.

Distribution: RKO. 7 reels.

Directors: Paul L. Stein, E.J. Babille (assistant director—uncredited), Bert Gilroy (assistant director—uncredited), Harry Joe Brown (additional sequences—uncredited), Horace Jackson (additional sequences—uncredited), Val Paul (additional sequences—uncredited), Ken Frank (additional scenes), C.T. Pyle (additional scenes).

Producers: Harry Joe Brown, Charles R. Rogers.

Writers: Thilde Förster (story), Guy Fowler (novel), Horace Jackson, Charles E. Whittaker.

Cinematography: Hal Mohr, Arthur C. Miller (uncredited).

Editing: Daniel Mandell.

Art director: Carroll Clark.

Costumes: Gwen Wakeling.

Sound: Earl A. Wolcott.

Music director: Arthur Lange.

Song: "Paradise" by Nacio Herb Brown.

Cast

Pola Negri (Madame Maria Draga), Roland Young (King Alexander), Basil Rathbone (Capt. Alex Pastitsch), H. B. Warner (Col. Stradimirovitsch), Anthony Bushell (Lieut. Iwan Petrovitch), Reginald Owen (Prime Minister), May Boley (Mascha), Frank Reicher (The General), George Baxter (Chedo), David Newell (Adjutant), Cleo Louise Borden (Crown Prince Milan), Frank Beek (Major Domo), Frank Dunn (servant), Carl Stockdale (Priest—uncredited), Lorimer Johnson (Minister), Paul Porcasi (Nightclub Proprietor—uncredited), Max Lucke (uncredited), Lillian Ward (uncredited), Allan Cavan (uncredited), Charles McMurphy (uncredited).

Synopsis

Captain Alex Pastitsch of Serbia has incurred large debts trying to keep his lover, Maria, in luxury, and now his military career is threatened. His superior, Col. Stradimirovitsch, begs Maria to leave Alex. She agrees, pretending to be interested in another man and, unbeknown to Alex, repays his debts. Then Maria returns to her former life as a cabaret dancer, becoming an enormous success. While performing, she attracts the attention of King Alexander, the Serbian ruler. She agrees to accompany the King back to the palace, extracting a promise from him to discover where Alex is. The drunken ruler is upset when Maria refuses to go to bed with him and has one of his officers take her home. The officer turns out to be Alex, who is stunned by seeing Maria, assuming the worst. Alex insults her and she attempts to flee to Vienna but is removed from the train and brought back to the king. He proposes marriage; Maria, realizing the power she would have, accepts. At a military parade, Alex refuses to salute the new queen and is imprisoned. Finally, after nearly a year of Maria's pleading for Alex's release, the king grants her wish and he is reinstated in the guard. The king's marriage causes unrest in the kingdom, and revolutionaries, including Alex, bomb the cathedral where their son, Milan, is to be christened. The palace is stormed and Mascha, the queen's servant, takes Milan away. The king is killed and Peter Georgevitch is installed. Col. Stradimirovitsch tells Alex to have Maria sign abdication papers but Alex informs her that this will declare her son a bastard. She refuses. The colonel orders her brought before a firing squad but moments before her execution, he decides to spare Maria and let her live in exile with Alex. Maria and Alex then join Mascha and Milan in a neighboring country.

Reviews

Announcement that Mayor Walker would introduce Pola Negri before the screening of her first talking picture, *A Woman Commands*, last night attracted tremendous crowds to the Mayfair. In most of the sequences, Miss Negri is attractive. Her accent is strongly foreign and her voice is a contralto. She sings and hums a song which drew applause from the crowded house. Although the picture, which boasts a beautiful cabaret entertainer, an impecunious guards officer and an impulsive king, is no masterpiece, it has several good episodes. The dénouement is very tame, but there is always the acting of Roland Young, Basil Rathbone and H. B. Warner, besides Miss Negri.

—*The New York Times*, January 29, 1932

115. Rathbone, Negri in *A Woman Commands*.

Pola Negri's return to the screen has been honored by Pathé with all the resources of the studio. As the café entertainer who manages to marry a weakling king, she brings the grand manner back to the screen, where it has been woefully lacking of late. And she not only speaks well with only a trace of accent, but she surprises us by singing with a throaty, untrained sweetness. If you like romance *really romantic,* you will revel in this picture.

—*Motion Picture Magazine*, March 1932

Pola Negri makes her talkie début here as a cabaret girl who becomes a queen. And if the costume vehicle chosen isn't entirely satisfactory, at least Pola proves that she may be greater in sound than she was in silence. Her voice is unusually pleasing.

—*Modern Screen*, April 1932

Hurrah! The queen of them all is back and more gorgeously beautiful, more glamorous, than ever. Whom do I mean? Who else but Pola Negri? Her vivid brunetteness is a welcome relief from the recent tidal wave of blondes, and her passion and fire are more than welcome after all this restrained, lackadaisical acting of the cigarette-flicking epigram school … And watch out for that voice of hers. It thrills one through and through to hear it, and it completely suits Pola. It's the kind of voice you'd expect her to have—deep and husky and full of emotion, and golden as a bell. I sat through *A Woman Commands* twice, especially to hear it. Pola is simply grand.

—Letter from a fan (L. B. D., Fort Worth, Texas) in *Picture Play*, June 1932

Hi Diddle Diddle

116. *Hi Diddle Diddle*, 1943.

L-R: Barton Hepburn, Billie Burke, Martha Scott, Dennis O'Keefe, Negri, Walter Kingsford

Released August 20, 1943. Andrew Stone Productions.

Distribution: United Artists Corporation. 8 reels.

Directors: Andrew L. Stone, Henry Kessler (assistant director).

Producers: Andrew L. Stone, Edward F. Finney (associate producer), Carley Harriman (assistant to producer).

Writers: Andrew L. Stone (original story), Frederick J. Jackson (screenplay), Edmund L. Hartmann.

Cinematography: Charles Edgar Schoenbaum.

Editor: Harvey Manger.

Art director: Frank Paul Sylos.

Set design: Earl Wooden.

Costumes: Adrian.

Makeup: Ted Larsen.

Sound: William H. Lynch.

Music director: Phil Boutelje.

Animation: Richard Bickenbach (uncredited), Ken Champin (uncredited), Gerry Chiniquy (uncredited), Gil Turner (uncredited), Owen Fitzgerald (layout artist—uncredited).

Cast

Adolphe Menjou (Col. Hector Phyffe), Martha Scott (Janie Prescott Phyffe), Pola Negri (Genya Smetana), Dennis O'Keefe (Sonny Phyffe), Billie Burke (Liza Prescott), Walter Kingsford (Sen. Jimmy Simpson), Barton Hepburn (Peter Warrington III), Georges Metaxa (Tony Spinelli), Eddie Marr (Michael Angelo, Croupier), Paul Porcasi (Impresario), Bert Roach (Husband, Taxi Cab Bit), Chick Chandler (Saunders, Hector's Chauffeur), Lorraine Miller (Director's Friend), Marek Windheim (Pianist), Richard Hageman (Boughton), Ellen Lowe (Flory, the Maid), Barry Macollum (Angus, the Club Cashier), Joe Devlin (Dan Hannigan, Bartender), Hal K. Dawson (Dr. Agnew, the Minister), Andrew Tombes (Mike, the Doorman), Byron Foulger (Watson, the Brokerage Firm Clerk), Ann Hunter (Sandra), June Havoc (Leslie Quayle), Bobby Barber (Saloon Waiter—uncredited), Don Brodie (George Bronson—uncredited), Jack Carr (Bill, the Bartender—uncredited), Jack Chefe (Waiter—uncredited), Kernan Cripps (Brokerage Firm Guard—uncredited), Bess Flowers (Wedding Guest—uncredited), Jack Gardner (First Reporter—uncredited), Jody Gilbert (Agitated Wife—uncredited), Buddy Gorman (Brokerage Firm Office Boy—uncredited), Mike Lally (Roulette Player—uncredited), Matt McHugh (Second Reporter—uncredited), Harold Miller (Wedding Guest—uncredited), Sidney Miller (Benny—uncredited), Neyle Morrow (Newsboy—uncredited), Henry Norton (Wedding Guest—uncredited), Tom Quinn (Brokerage Firm Employee—uncredited), Harry Tyler (Brokerage Firm Teller—uncredited), Leonard Walker (Conductor—uncredited).

Synopsis

As Janie Prescott is about to marry Sonny Phyffe, her mother announces she is broke because Janie's former suitor, Peter Warrington III, lost all her money in junk investments and gambling. Sonny doesn't care about Janie's inheritance and marries her anyway. Sonny's father, Col. Hector Phyffe, shows up pretending to be a wealthy investor, but he's actually a charming con artist living on an allowance from his new wife, temperamental opera diva Genya Smetana. Hector drags Sonny away after the wedding to recoup Mrs. Prescott's fortune by playing a roulette wheel rigged with the help of club singer Leslie. Then he embroils the naïve Sonny in a scheme to swindle Peter with worthless stocks. Father and son are repeatedly caught in compromising circumstances, and Hector's quickly improvised cover stories dig them both deeper into trouble, especially with the jealous Genya. When Hector presents their ill-gotten gains to Mrs. Prescott, she and Peter admit they had only pretended her fortune was lost, to test Sonny's love for Janie. The misunderstandings are sorted out, and the newlyweds finally get a chance to be alone behind closed doors. The rest of the company closes by wailing a *Tannhauser* aria around Genya's piano, prompting the Wagnerian characters on her wallpaper to cringe and flee.

Reviews

A delightful screwball comedy with a most unusual cast: Adolphe Menjou, Martha Scott, Pola Negri, Dennis O'Keefe, Billie Burke and June Havoc. Among the uncrediteds are Bess Flowers, Don Brodie, and Lou Costello's pal Bobby Barber. This was silent-era star Negri's next-to-last film, Disney's *The Moon-Spinners* (1964) being her final movie. Here she's hilarious as a pompous Wagnerian opera diva with a voice that penetrates your head like a nail. Whenever Madame Genya Smetana starts to warble, Adolphe Menjou (as Col. Hector Phyffe, an elegant con man) finds a way to escape the noisy onslaught. The colonel's son, played by Dennis O'Keefe, is marrying Martha Scott, the daughter of scatterbrained society dame Billie Burke, who confesses that she's been swindled out of $50K. Menjou is determined to get back this money, which was lost at a crooked gambling joint, and he enlists the aid of June Havoc, a tall, exotic-looking club singer/dancer. Watch for Havoc's spotlight moment when she stands next to a 7 foot tall Panoram, a big-screen-TV-like, coin-fed contraption that shows musical film clips on demand. June backs up a singing "Soundie" of herself with some jazzy harmony and footwork. Perhaps the best technical gimmick comes at the end. Negri screeches, Menjou winces, and illustrations that are duplicated dozens of times on the wallpaper come to life and all run away simultaneously. A fine end to a fun picture! The cast makes the most of some sharp dialogue by Bob Hope's long-time scriptwriter Edmund L. Hartmann.
     —Annie Van Auken, Amazon.com

From the first frame to the final fadeout, *Hi Diddle Diddle*, Andrew Stone's initial United Artists release, which he produced and directed as well, appears to have but one motive, to convulse the customers, and it succeeds admirably in this respect. Marking the return of svelte Pola Negri to American films, the picture also boasts the presence of Adolphe

Menjou and Billie Burke. Miss Negri is cast here as a temperamental prima donna with a Wagnerian complex. Menjou is her recently acquired husband, who has lost some of his independence by having to live on her bounty, but not his eye for the gals …

Leon Schlesinger provides a hilarious animated cartoon wallpaper sequence to accompany the combined warblings of Pola Negri, Billie Burke, June Havoc, and four newspaper reporters in a Wagnerian finale.

    —*Motion Picture Daily*, July 29, 1943

It's the old bedroom farce of the newly married couple who, for the most outlandish reasons, can't seem to get together. It's as far-fetched as the moon, tickly as champagne bubbles, and heavy as a feather. But it's just what the old medico ordered after a surfeit of heavy war dramas … Adolphe Menjou, [Dennis] O'Keefe's father, and Pola Negri, his stepmother, are a perfect team. June Havoc sings rather well. All in all, it's better than a day at the funhouse and not nearly so strenuous. Your reviewer says: Whoopee!

    —*Photoplay*, November 1943

The Moon-Spinners

Released July 8, 1964. Walt Disney Productions.

Distribution: Buena Vista. 2 reels.

Director: James Neilson.

Producers: Walt Disney (uncredited), Bill Anderson (co-producer), Hugh Attwooll (associate producer).

Writers: Michael Dyne (screenplay), Mary Stewart (book).

Cinematography: Paul Beeson.

Art director: Anthony Masters.

Costumes: Anthony Mendleson.

Editing: Gordon Stone.

Makeup: Harry Frampton, A.G. Scott (hairdressing).

Art department: John Graysmark (uncredited).

Sound: Jonathan Bates.

Special Effects: Jimmy Harris (uncredited), Garth Inns (uncredited), Jimmy Ward (uncredited), Jack Woodbridge (uncredited).

Stunts: Cliff Diggins (uncredited).

Camera Operator: David Harcourt.

Music: Ron Grainer.

Animals: Jimmy Chipperfield.

Cast

Hayley Mills (Nikky Ferris), Eli Wallach (Stratos), Peter McEnery (Mark Camford), Joan Greenwood (Aunt Frances Ferris), Irene Papas (Sophia), John Le Mesurier (Anthony Gamble), Paul Stassino (Lambis), Sheila Hancock (Cynthia Gamble), Michael Davis (Alexis), André Morell (Yacht Captain), George Pastell (Police Lieutenant), Tutte Lemkow (Orestes), Steve Lemkow (Hearse Driver), Harry Tardios (Bus Driver), Pamela Barrie (Ariadne), Pola Negri (Madame Habib), Terry Gilkyson (Singer—uncredited).

Synopsis

Vacationing in Crete with her aunt, seventeen-year-old Nikky learns that their reservations at the Moon-Spinners Hotel have not been recognized, but hostile owners Stratos and his sister Sophia reluctantly give them a room. They meet Mark, a young British expatriate who is in a running feud with Stratos. Nikky is attracted to Mark and becomes involved when she finds him wounded in a deserted church after being ambushed and shot by Lambis, Stratos's cohort. Her complicity uncovered, she is imprisoned by Stratos but is rescued by Mark and Sophia's son, Alexis. Nikky learns that Mark was sacked from his job as a messenger for a London bank because of a jewel robbery which he believes Stratos committed. The couple then encounters Anthony Gamble, who, as Stratos's partner, is planning to sell the jewels to Madame Habib, a millionaire. These revelations send Mark on a chase after Stratos, while Nikky appeals to Madame. Following a struggle, the police board Madame's yacht and apprehend Stratos as Mark is exonerated.

Reviews

Disney's race against time to find adequate vehicles for the popular but fast-growing Hayley Mills is nearing its end as she turns woman, but he'll get plenty of mileage and good returns from this Grecian gambol… Pola Negri makes a late entrance as a weird, wealthy widow type who gets her kicks from jewels. It's rather obvious novelty casting, and the part isn't likely to tee off a new screen career for the silent-screen siren. She looks appropriately exotic and sounds (naturally or dubbed?) like a road company Maria Ouspenskaya.

—*Variety*, June 1964

Eli Wallach commented that this film was not Disney's typical family-oriented fare. He thought Mrs. Disney had liked *The Moon-Spinners* book and had urged Walt to buy it and make it into a movie.

Filming in Crete was very enjoyable for Wallach except for the long shooting schedule and separation from his family. On days off, he would go sightseeing.

I also like the climax, in which the frantic young heroine, chasing after her briefly kidnapped hero, finds herself aboard a luxurious yacht occupied by an Oriental heiress who has a majestic leopard for a pet. Such luxury as this recalls the old days. And so does the heiress, who is played by Pola Negri, the silent-film temptress. This is appropriately droll. Indeed, if there had been more of this in the script, done by Michael Dyne from a novel by Mary Stewart, and if the director, James Neilson, had allowed Mr. Wallach, Joan Greenwood and others to play as broadly as they seem to want, this might have turned out to be a melodrama with a bright tinge of adult spoof. As it stands, it is a lively diversion, easy and obvious, for the young.

—*The New York Times*, November 4, 1964

ACKNOWLEDGMENTS

THERE ARE MANY individuals to thank for this book. Many acquaintances of Miss Negri came through with material, knowledge and expertise about her life and career.

First and foremost, I thank Michael Heinrich in Germany for his many years of encouragement, material, photos, and, most of all, believing in this project. Kevin Brownlow took time out of his consistently busy schedule to answer my many emails and give invaluable feedback and information. Most of the details presented in sidebars in the Filmography section were supplied by Mr. Brownlow. Loretta Ellerbee, Negri's caretaker in the 1980s, was amazing and has become a wonderful friend. Colleen Hailey at Binghamton University's Glenn G. Bartle Library always responded with as much enthusiasm as I have. The Margaret Herrick Library in Beverly Hills sent me the Negri microfiche files from which I drew heavily, including sourced and non-sourced clippings and articles. Michelle Sullivan and Laurel Hirsch were marvelous researchers and supplied me with material I could not have acquired by myself.

Other important contributions came from the late Larry Ashmead, Negri's publisher and friend, who said, "Write the book;" Jim Craig for kindly making me a copy of Margaret West's Last Will and Testament; Gene Czebiniak for his amazing cover art; the late Gilbert Denman, Negri's attorney; Neal Hart (grandson to silent-film star Neal Hart); Alfred Allan Lewis, Negri's incredible ghostwriter; and George Schoenbrunn, whose personal correspondences I drew heavily upon. Others in a long list include the late Priscilla Bonner, Diana Serra Cary (Baby Peggy), Tom Cook, the late Jean Darling, Joop van Dijk, Uwe Klöchner-Draga, John Drennon, Lynne Epstein, the late Doug Fairbanks, Jr., the late Leatrice Gilbert Fountain, the late June Havoc, Lydia Herzel, Jeff Hockenheimer, Gray Horan, the late Josephine Hutchinson, Margaret King Stanley, Johanna von Koczian, Marina Loos, Mary Anita Loos, the late A. C. Lyles, Frank Noack, the late Anita Page, Gary Pedro, Brenda Rhodes, Maria Riva, Budd Schulberg, Lisa Stein, the late Andrew Stone, the late Eli Wallach, Kordian W. Wichtowski, and the late Billy Wilder.

I am indebted to Stephen Spero for his copy editing and to Linda Bonney Olin for her masterful guidance. All of these generous people, and those I have inadvertently left out, have my deep gratitude.

Finally, I thank God for His goodness and His help to bring this book to fruition.

A Note on Research

When possible, I have included within the text the appropriate source of information (*New York Times*, *Motion Picture Magazine*, etc.), unless the article or material was either cut off or unsourced. I drew on hundreds of clippings and articles from the Margaret Herrick Library, books listed in the bibliography, and material collected over the years by myself or generously copied for me by others. In addition to interviews I conducted, the internet's most valuable movie reference site, the IMDb, and the American Film Institute were indispensable, as were back issues of *Variety* and early movie fan magazines supplied by the Media History Digital Library.

Quoted material is an accurate transcription of what was written in books and magazines. Occasionally authors would try to capture Negri's accent, and those quotes are written as they appeared in print.

I was able to view some fine prints of Negri's silent films on either VHS or DVD. At the George Eastman House in Rochester, New York, I viewed quality prints of her *Madame DuBarry*, *Carmen,* and *Forbidden Paradise.* Mr. Heinrich and Mr. Schoenbrunn also sent me video tapes of some of Negri's early German cinema as well as cassette tapes of vocal recordings she made on discs.

It has not been possible in every case to determine the original source and copyright status of old article clippings and photographs used in this book. If I have inadvertently included material that is currently under copyright, please forward detailed information to my publisher address.

BIBLIOGRAPHY

Amberg, George. *The New York Times Film Reviews: 1913–1970*. New York: Arno Press, 1971.

Ardmore, Jane. *The Self-Enchanted: Mae Murray: Image of an Era*. New York: McGraw-Hill, 1959.

Beinhorn, Courtenay Wyche. "Pola Negri—Tempestuous Temptress." *Take One*, September 1978, 35–46.

Bellamy, Madge. *A Darling of the Twenties*. Vestal, NY: Vestal Press, 1989.

Belletti, Valeria. *Adventures of a Hollywood Secretary: Her Private Letters from Inside the Studios of the 1920's*. Ed. Cari Beauchamp. Los Angeles: University of California Press, 2006.

Berle, Milton, and Haskel Frankel. *An Autobiography*. New York: Delacorte Press, 1974.

Blum, Daniel. *A Pictorial History of the Silent Screen*. New York: Grosset & Dunlap, 1953.

Brooks, Louise. *Lulu in Hollywood*. New York: Alfred A. Knopf, 1982.

Brownlow, Kevin. *The Parade's Gone By*. Los Angeles: University of California Press, 1968.

Card, James. *Seductive Cinema—The Art of Silent Film*. New York: Alfred A. Knopf, 1994.

Carr, Larry. *Four Fabulous Faces—Swanson, Garbo, Crawford, Dietrich*. New York: Galahad Books, 1970.

Chaplin, Charles. *My Autobiography*. New York: Simon and Schuster, 1964.

Chaplin, Lita Grey, and Morton Cooper. *My Life with Chaplin*. New York: Bernard Geis Associates, 1966.

Cooper, Miriam, and Bonnie Herndon. *Dark Lady of the Silents—My Life in Early Hollywood*. New York: The Bobbs-Merrill Company, Inc., 1973.

Davies, Marion. *The Times We Had*. Ed. Kenneth S. Marx and Pamela Pfau. New York: Ballantine Books, 1975.

Everson, William K. *American Silent Film*. New York: Da Capo Press, 1998.

——. *Love in the Film*. Secaucus, NJ: Citadel Press, 1979.

Eyman, Scott. *Ernst Lubitsch: Laughter in Paradise*. New York: Simon & Schuster, 1993.

——. *The Speed of Sound*. New York: Simon & Schuster, 1997.

——. *Mary Pickford: America's Sweetheart*. New York: Donald I. Fine, Inc., 1990.

Geduld, Harry M. *The Birth of Talkies*. Bloomington: Indiana University Press, 1975.

Gish, Lillian, and Ann Pinchot. *The Movies, Mr. Griffith and Me*. Englewood Cliffs, NJ: Prentice-Hall, Inc., 1969.

Godowsky, Dagmar. *First Person Plural*. New York: The Viking Press, 1958.

Griffith, Richard, and Arthur Mayer. *The Movies*. New York: Simon & Schuster, 1970.

Hopper, Hedda. *From Under My Hat*. Garden City, NY: Doubleday & Company, Inc., 1952.

Hopper, Hedda, and James Brough. *The Whole Truth and Nothing But*. Garden City, NY: Doubleday & Company, Inc., 1963.

Hull, David Stewart. *Film in the Third Reich: A Study of German Cinema 1933–1945.* Los Angeles: University of California Press, 1969.

Katz, Ephraim. *The Film Encyclopedia.* New York: Thomas Y. Crowell, 1979.

Kobal, John. *Gods & Goddesses of the Movies.* New York: Crescent Books, 1973.

Kreimeier, Klaus. *The UFA Story.* Los Angeles: University of California Press, 1999.

Kreuder, Peter. *Nur Puppen haben keine Tränen.* Munich: Deutscher Taschenbuch Verlag GmbH & Co. KG., 2003.

Lambert, Gavin. *Nazimova—A Biography.* New York: Alfred A. Knopf, 1997.

Lasky, Jesse L., and Don Weldon. *I Blow My Own Horn.* Garden City, NY: Doubleday & Company, Inc., 1957.

Leider, Emily W. *Dark Lover.* New York: Farrar, Straus and Giroux, 2003.

Loos, Anita. *Kiss Hollywood Good-By.* New York: The Viking Press, 1974.

———. *The Talmadge Girls.* New York: The Viking Press, 1978.

Menjou, Adolphe, and M. M. Musselman. *It Took Nine Tailors.* New York: McGraw-Hill Book Company, Inc., 1948.

Moeller, Felix. *The Film Minister—Goebbels and Cinema in the Third Reich.* Stuttgart: Edition Axel Menges, 2000.

Moore, Colleen. *Silent Star.* Garden City, NY: Doubleday & Company, Inc., 1968.

Morris, Michael. *Madame Valentino—The Many Lives of Natacha Rambova.* New York: Abbeville Press, 1991.

Negra, Diane. "Immigrant Stardom in Imperial America: Pola Negri and the Problem of Typology." *Camera Obscura* 48.159 (2001).

Negri, Pola. *Memoirs of a Star.* Garden City, NY: Doubleday & Company, Inc., 1970.

Robinson, David. *Chaplin—His Life and Art.* New York: McGraw-Hill Publishing Company, 1985.

Rosen, Marjorie. *Popcorn Venus.* New York: Avon, 1974.

Scagnetti, Jack. *The Intimate Life of Rudolph Valentino.* New York: Jonathan David Publishers, Inc., 1975.

Schulman, Irving. *Valentino.* New York: Trident Press, 1967.

Shearer, Stephen Michael. *Gloria Swanson—The Ultimate Star.* New York: Thomas Dunne Books, 2013.

Stenn, David. *Clara Bow—Runnin' Wild.* New York: Doubleday, 1988.

Swanson, Gloria. *Swanson on Swanson.* New York: Simon & Schuster, 1980.

Ullman, S. George. *Valentino As I Knew Him.* New York: A. L. Burt Company, 1926.

Villecco, Tony. *Silent Stars Speak—Interviews with Twelve Cinema Pioneers.* Jefferson, NC: McFarland & Company, Inc., 2001.

Wanger, Walter. *You Must Remember This.* New York: G.P. Putnam's Sons, 1975.

Walker, Alexander. *The Shattered Silents*. New York: William Morrow and Company, Inc., 1979.

Werner, Paul. *Die Skandalchronik des deutschen Films*. Frankfurt am Main: Fischer Taschenbuch Verlag, 1990.

Zierold, Norman J. *Sex Goddesses of the Silent Screen*. Chicago: Henry Regnery Company, 1973.

Zolotow, Maurice. *Billy Wilder in Hollywood*. New York: G.P. Putnam's Sons, 1977.

LIST OF PHOTOGRAPHS

INDEX

ABOUT THE AUTHOR

117. Tony Villecco

Tony Villecco earned a B. A. degree in English literature and creative writing from Binghamton University and studied with poetess Ruth Stone. A classically trained tenor, he has studied voice with internationally renowned soprano Virginia Zeani and received praise from legendary operatic tenor Nicolai Gedda. He has performed a wide range of musical theatre, oratorio, and opera, as well as the great jazz vocals of the 30's, 40's, and 50's. He appeared at Greenwich Village's historic Rose's Turn and Manhattan's Don't Tell Mama.

Mr. Villecco's articles have appeared in *Classical Singer Magazine*, *School Music News*, *Classic Images*, and the *Binghamton Press and Sun-Bulletin*. He serves as an arts reviewer with Broome Arts Mirror. His first book, *Silent Stars Speak—Interviews with Twelve Cinema Pioneers*, was released to critical acclaim in 2001 by McFarland and Company, Inc.

Praise for *Pola Negri—The Hollywood Years*:

"An engaging, well researched biography of one of the silent screen's most luminous stars."
—Emily W. Leider, biographer/writer (*Dark Lover: The Life and Death of Rudolph Valentino; Becoming Mae West; Myrna Loy: The Only Good Girl in Hollywood*)

Praise for *Silent Stars Speak—Interviews with Twelve Cinema Pioneers:*

"Seriously worth your time . . . Excellent, entertaining, and well written with great photos"
—*Classic Images*

"Wonderful . . . important . . . extensive filmography . . . dozens of rare stills . . . worthy"
—*Film & History*

"Impeccable [research] . . . The rare stills and detailed filmographies . . . are excellent."
—*Film Review*

"I learned more about Francis Lederer, Louise Brooks, Virginia Cherrill, and their experiences with Reinhardt, Pabst, Kortner, Chaplin, than in any other biography I've ever read."
—Eli Wallach, actor